# INTERNATIONAL SOCIAL PROGRESS

# INTERNATIONAL SOCIAL PROGRESS

## THE WORK OF THE INTERNATIONAL LABOUR ORGANISATION *of the* LEAGUE OF NATIONS

BY

## G. A. JOHNSTON

M.A., D.Phil., sometime Lecturer in Philosophy in the
Universities of Glasgow and St. Andrews

LONDON: GEORGE ALLEN & UNWIN LTD.
RUSKIN HOUSE, 40 MUSEUM STREET, W.C. 1

*First published in 1924*

*Printed in Great Britain by*
UNWIN BROTHERS, LIMITED, LONDON AND WOKING

# PREFACE

THIS book, after an analysis of the conditions of social progress, endeavours to explain the part that is being played by the International Labour Organisation of the League of Nations in the general movement of social development throughout the world, and examines the contributions which the Organisation has been able to make to constructive social reform. Its main purpose is to give a plain account of that work. Four years have now elapsed since the Organisation established by Part XIII of the Peace Treaty began to function, and there has therefore been time to attempt some survey of its activities and some estimate of the value of its achievements. To one who, like the author, has been concerned from the start with the organisation and development of the International Labour Office, the passage of time has brought a gradually deepening conviction that this Organisation, founded in a spirit of generous enthusiasm, is destined, amid all the sombre difficulties of the post-war world, to fulfil a function of gradually increasing importance in the maintenance of that international peace which is based on social justice.

I should perhaps add that this book is a personal contribution to the annals of social progress ; it is not an official history of the Organisation, and the International Labour Office is not responsible for any expression of opinion contained in it.

G. A. JOHNSTON.

GENEVA,
*March* 23, 1924.

# CONTENTS

# International Social Progress

## CHAPTER I

## INTRODUCTORY: THE CONDITIONS OF SOCIAL PROGRESS

IT has become a fashion to criticise the industrial order of civilisation in which we live. In Italy, in France, in Germany, and in Great Britain itself, loud warnings are being uttered that, owing to the disintegration of its industrial basis, the whole fabric of civilisation is in process of decay and dissolution. The prophet and the philosopher, with an analysis as superficial as the problem is profound, proclaim that the diseases of the modern world are due to the industrial order, and draw the conclusion that the industrial order must give place to something else.

Now all progress must be realised in the conditions under which ordinary men and women live and work. The industrial order is the order in which we live, and if the conditions in which we live are to be improved, if social progress is to be realised, it must be within the system which actually exists.

But is the industrial order essentially vicious? [1] To reply in the affirmative would suggest a misreading of the whole course of history. Social progress has consisted primarily in the extension to ever-increasing numbers of people of facilities for the pursuit of objects

---

[1] By the industrial order, I mean the system under which commodities are produced by labour specialised and organised to operate machinery on a large scale. I am not concerned in this book with the question whether the system of control within the industrial order should be socialistic or capitalistic.

9

not necessary for mere survival. In a primitive community all activities are immediately directed to the survival of the individual and the race. Social progress depends on the production and still more on the will to the production of a *surplus*—something more than is directly necessary for the avoidance of death through starvation. In the history of the world this *surplus* first began to be produced by agriculture in the deltas of great rivers, such as the Nile. This surplus was enough to render possible the creation of a small leisured class. This in turn led to the invention of writing, architecture, mathematics and other arts and sciences necessary to social progress. But, until the industrial revolution, the number of people who could enjoy and further such progress was extremely small, because labour was sufficiently productive to produce only a relatively small surplus over what it needed to ensure mere survival. Now, owing to the immense increase in the output of labour resulting from the use of machinery and the development of large-scale production, the surplus produced is extremely large. Whether this surplus is equitably distributed between the various agents in production is a question with which it is not the purpose of this book to deal. We are only concerned here to emphasise the fact that this distributable surplus which is the material condition of all social progress is available only in the industrial order.

Under the industrial system, the production of the elementary necessaries of life requires only a tithe of the time involved in a primitive community. The rest of the time of the industrial community can be, and is, devoted to the manufacture of luxuries or to the enjoyment of leisure. The industrial system is the condition of the emancipation of man from the bondage of Nature, the steady pressure of rudimentary needs. Now this freedom, this leisure, is another essential condition of social progress. And it is possible only under the industrial order.

But the industrial order has a further characteristic. Although it increases the freedom of the individual in relation to Nature, it diminishes his freedom in relation to the community. In a pre-industrial society most men produce what is required for their own needs and consume what they produce. But in the industrial order men rarely produce what they themselves consume. They are therefore dependent on the community both to give them the opportunity to produce at all, and to give them commodities to consume.

As the industrial order develops, the individual community or State loses the self-sufficiency which it possessed under a simpler regime. As in a primitive pre-industrial community the individual produces almost all that he himself consumes, so in a rudimentary industrial community the community as a whole produces almost all that it consumes. But in an era of highly developed industrialism such as that in which we now live, each nation is dependent on the community of nations both to enable it to dispose of what it produces and to obtain in exchange commodities for consumption. The industrial order, in its development, essentially involves international relations.

These international relations of modern industry are to be found on two different levels. On the one hand, great international trusts have been established for the production and marketing of such things as oil, meat and tobacco. On the other hand, the simplest manufactured article is international in its composition. In the coat that I wear the wool probably came from Australia, the buttons from Czechoslovakia, the thread from Scotland and the dyes from Germany. In these two respects, then, modern industry is essentially international.

Now the international character of modern industry involves intense competition. If oil can be produced more cheaply in California than in Roumania, the Roumanian wells may have to cease operation: if buttons can be produced more cheaply in Belgium than in Czechoslovakia, then the Czechoslovak manufacturers will ultimately have to close down. Owing to the intensity of this competition, manufacturers in one country cannot take any step which would result in raising the cost of production unless they have some agreement with manufacturers in all other countries with which they compete that they will adopt similar measures.

It is this intense internationalism of modern industry which has logically led to the conclusion that for the diseases of the modern industrial order, themselves international, international remedies must be sought. However anxious one State may be to improve the conditions under which its workpeople labour, it is impossible for it, owing to the fear of international competition, to adopt reforms without having an assurance that other industrial States will take similar action.

The classical example of the adoption of an international remedy for an international disease of modern industry is the prohibition of the use of white phosphorus in the manufacture of matches. Matches used to be made of white phosphorus, which is poisonous, and produces in the workers exposed to it a terrible disease. It was known that matches could equally well be made of red phosphorus, which is chemically identical, but is not poisonous. While it was universally recognised that it would be desirable to use red phosphorus and not white phosphorus, great hesitation was shown in taking this step, because red phosphorus is slightly more expensive than white. If any State with an international trade in matches had prohibited the use of white phosphorus, its own industry would have been driven out of the international market, and its workers would have been saved from the risk of disease and death from phosphorus poisoning at the expense of the risk of disease and death from unemployment and starvation.

It therefore became clear that the only remedy was an international remedy. Only if *all* States would agree to prohibit the use of white phosphorus would it be possible to get *any* State to do it. It was realised that the only real solution of such international difficulties was an international solution. The diseases involved in social progress, which was essentially international, would tend to destroy the whole fabric unless remedies could be applied on an international basis.

An international solution was, in fact, applied, before the War, in the case of the prohibition of the use of white phosphorus in the manufacture of matches. This solution was reached in 1906, but only after infinite negotiation and as a result of two special international conferences. It was obvious that if such special negotiations had to be undertaken in every individual case in which there was a general desire to secure international improvement, progress would be impossibly slow. The great need was for permanent machinery which would enable the countries of the world to come together regularly and automatically for the discussion of industrial improvements which all desired but few or none were able to introduce without the agreement of all.

This need was greatly emphasised by the War. The War made clear, even to those who had been blind before, the economic interdependence of the nations of the world. It threw a new light on the international ramifications of industry and finance, and revealed to many for the first time the international relations of trade unions and the importance of the part played by labour in production. Men began to realise that in the last resort the bonds, economic, social and humane, that unite nations are more potent than the disintegrating forces which drag them asunder ; and that nations, however self-sufficient they may appear, can exist only by co-operating with other nations.

It was in these circumstances that it was decided to incorporate in the Treaty of Peace the constitution of a permanent organisation which would supply the machinery for the constant consideration of conditions of labour from an international standpoint.

It is the purpose of this book to examine the part which the International Labour Organisation, thus established by Part XIII of the Peace Treaty, is called upon to play in the adventure of constructive internationalism to which the modern world is consciously or unconsciously committed.

## CHAPTER II

## THE ORIGINS OF INTERNATIONAL LABOUR LEGISLATION

EVERY institution has its roots in the past. The International Labour Organisation, while it constitutes an exception to many rules, has conformed to this principle. But it is equally true that no institution is fully explained by its history. Again the International Labour Organisation exemplifies this truth. It is misleading to regard the International Labour Organisation merely as the outcome of previous endeavours, merely as the culmination of earlier efforts. It is, however, essential, if the work of the Organisation is to be justly appreciated, that some attention should be paid to the genesis and development of the idea of international labour legislation.

There is a real process of evolution between the visions of Robert Owen and the International Labour Organisation as it exists to-day, but though the evolution is there, it is not a continuous evolution. The International Labour Organisation is indeed a " discontinuous variation." Its birth was hastened by the world cataclysm of 1914-1918, but even if the Great War had not taken place, it would undoubtedly, under some form or another, and with greater or less delay, have been constituted. While it is a child of the War, its birth had already been prepared for by almost a century of effort.

By a curious coincidence, the Congress of Aix-la-Chapelle, which met almost exactly a century before the Paris Peace Conference and with a very similar purpose, was offered the opportunity of incorporating in its decisions, as the Paris Conference did, provisions relating to labour and industry. That Congress received a petition declaring that a prime task for the Governments of Europe was the international fixation of the legal limits of the normal work-day for the industrial classes of Europe. The petition was presented by Robert Owen, a British employer and social reformer, who also requested the Congress to appoint a Commission to report on the question. A chance had been given to history to anticipate itself—a chance which it did not accept.

No further attempt was made to translate into reality the ideals of international labour legislation until the year 1838–1839. In that year the French economist, Blanqui, in his *Cours d'économie industrielle,* impressed by the difficulties in the way of individual employers or even of all the employers in one nation instituting reforms in labour conditions, owing to the severity of international competition, proposed the conclusion of international treaties to regulate such conditions.

It was, however, left to an Alsatian manufacturer, Daniel Le Grand, to be the first after Owen to approach the Governments. After various efforts to move the French Government to introduce protective labour legislation, Le Grand sent in 1847 a petition to Paris, London, Berlin and Berne. The object of this petition is sufficiently indicated by its title :—

Respectful appeal addressed to the Governments of France, England, Prussia, the other German States, and Switzerland, with a view to the adoption of national laws and also international legislation for the protection of the working class against work excessive in amount and at too early an age, the primary and principal cause of its physical deterioration, its moral degradation and its deprivation of the blessings of family life.[1]

This memorial was received in the same spirit as those of Owen, but Le Grand persisted and addressed a further appeal to the Governments of the States of chief industrial importance. This appeal was published four times in the years 1853, 1855, 1856 and 1857.

[1] Mahaim : *Droit international ouvrier,* pp. 194–195.

In the case of a country such as Austria, which possessed little or no similar legislation, such negotiations would necessarily be attended with serious difficulties and delays. The Federal Council, in accordance with this proposal, addressed to the Swiss Legations at Paris, Berlin, Vienna and Rome, and the Swiss Consulates-General in London and Brussels, a note calling upon them to obtain from reliable sources confidential information of a character which would make it possible to know which States in Europe would co-operate in the matter of the international regulation of labour in factories. This action of the Swiss Government is of particular interest as being the first official attempt to attain some practical result in connection with international labour legislation.

It was not to be expected that the first attempt would succeed, and, in fact, it did not succeed. All the Governments interrogated expressed their views with the exception of Belgium, and all were more or less unfavourable. The British Government considered it impracticable to conclude an international convention on the subject of factory legislation. The reply from France indicated that in general the Government deemed it not within the province of the State to interfere with contracts between employers and employees, and the Government was therefore inclined *a fortiori* to adopt an attitude unfavourable to the international treatment of the matter. The Prussian Government was likewise unprepared to co-operate owing to its opposition to the regulation of labour conditions by treaties. The Italian and Austro-Hungarian Governments exhibited great reserve in their answers and asked, in effect, for more information with regard to the scope of such proposed international regulation.

The Swiss Government was naturally discouraged by this unfavourable reception of its initiative. It did not, however, abandon the ideal, and in the end its efforts were crowned with success.

The next country to show a practical interest in the development of international labour legislation was

France. After discussion had taken place at various small conferences, a group of French deputies submitted in 1885 to a Committee of the Chamber of Deputies a bill indicating willingness on the part of the French Government to comply with the overtures of the Swiss Government concerning international labour legislation, and readiness to assume the initiative in agreement with Switzerland in endeavouring to constitute a system of international law that would have as its aim the abolition of child labour under the age of fourteen, the limitation of the work of women and minors, and measures of hygiene and safety, accident insurance, inspection, a normal work-day, a weekly rest and an international bureau of labour statistics. This bill is of particular interest as including the first suggestion for the establishment of an international labour office. It is needless to say that this bill was not adopted. Is it not the fate of fruitful ideas to be rejected?

Interest in the question now passed to Germany. In the year 1886, members of the German Social Democratic Party developed a scheme with a view to the adoption by the Reichstag of a resolution asking that the Imperial Chancellor should convene a conference of the principal industrial States with a view to formulating a uniform basis for an international agreement for the protection of labour. The particular measures recommended were the legal establishment of a ten-hour working day, the suppression of night work, and the abolition of the work of children under fourteen years of age. The proposed resolution was of course defeated, but the heated discussions which took place gave publicity to the idea of international labour legislation. The realisation of this ideal was brought a stage nearer through the issue in Germany of two influential publications. One of these was *The Question of the International Protection of Labour*, by Dr. George Adler ; the other, *The International Regulation of Industry*, by Professor Brentano. These books examined in detail the possibility and the desirability of international regulation of industrial and labour conditions, and helped to lay the basis for the detailed schemes which were later put into operation.

In 1889 the Swiss Government considered that the time was now ripe for further action. It addressed a circular note to the Governments of Europe recalling to mind its previous unsuccessful action in 1881, and drawing attention to the progress that had been made in the education of public opinion in the intervening period of eight years. This note recognised the impossibility of obtaining agreement with regard to a comprehensive programme in one conference. It therefore proposed that an international conference should be called to deal solely with questions of the international regulation of Sunday work and the work of women and children. It was considered essential that before international conventions could be adopted on such questions an international conference should be held. The following States intimated that they were favourable to the suggestion of the Swiss Government : Austria-Hungary, Belgium, France, Holland, Luxemburg and Portugal. The replies of Great Britain and Italy contained reservations. Russia refused to participate. Denmark, Germany, Norway and Sweden sent no reply to the note, and Spain merely acknowledged receipt.

The intention of the Swiss Government had been to convene the Conference if possible in September 1889, but in view of the replies to her note it was decided to postpone the Conference till the following year. Another note was therefore addressed to the Powers which had previously been approached, which intimated that a detailed programme for the coming meeting would be transmitted to the Powers interested. This programme was duly submitted, together with an invitation to a Conference to be held in May 1890. The persistent efforts of the Swiss Government seemed to be about to be crowned with success, but at the eleventh hour the Government cancelled the Conference.

This sudden cancellation is one of the most dramatic incidents in the history of the development of international labour legislation. It was due to one of the sudden interventions of the German Emperor in international affairs. On February 4, 1890, i.e. three months before the International Conference convened by the Swiss Confederation, the German Emperor issued two rescripts. The first rescript was addressed to Bismarck and reads as follows :—

I am resolved to lend a hand to the betterment of the condition of the German workers in proportion to my solicitude occasioned by the necessity of maintaining German industry in such a state that it can meet the competition of the international market and insure thereby its own existence and that of the workers as well. The decadence of German industry, by the loss of foreign outlets, would deprive of their means of subsistence not only employers but also their employees. The difficulties which oppose themselves to the betterment of the condition of our workers and which result from international competition can be, if not surmounted, at least diminished, in no other way than by the international agreement of the countries which dominate the international market.

Being convinced that the other Governments are equally animated with the desire of submitting to a common examination the tentative proposals on the subject concerning which international negotiations have been broached by the workers of these countries, I want my official representatives in France, England, Belgium and Switzerland to find out whether the Governments are disposed to enter into negotiations with us with the aim of bringing about an international agreement on the possibility of giving satisfaction to the needs and desires of the workers which have found expression in the strikes of late years and in other forms of unrest.

As soon as my proposal shall be accepted in principle, I charge you to convoke all the Governments interested in like measure in the labour question, to take part in a conference which shall deliberate upon the questions raised.

BERLIN, *February* 4, 1890. WILLIAM.

The International Conference of 1890 prepared for with such persistence by Switzerland was duly held, not, however, at Berne, but at Berlin. Switzerland had acquiesced in the German hegemony of the movement. But had history?

In accordance with the Emperor's instructions, Bismarck lost no time in communicating to the Western

Powers an invitation to send delegates to a Labour Conference in Berlin. All the Powers originally invited by Switzerland were approached with the exception of Russia. The Emperor also communicated the programme of the Conference to Pope Leo XIII, with a request for aid and sanction. The Pope, in reply, endorsed the aims of the Conference.

The Conference assembled on March 15, 1890. It consisted of representatives of fourteen countries, namely, Austria-Hungary, Belgium, Denmark, Great Britain, France, Germany, Holland, Italy, Luxemburg, Norway, Spain, Switzerland and Sweden. The President was Baron Berlepsch, the Imperial Minister of Commerce. Baron Berlepsch, in his inaugural address, struck the note that was to be followed by the Conference. He referred to the menace which had arisen from industrial competition between States, and thus justified the attempt that was being made to realise an agreement between the Governments in order to obviate the common dangers which resulted from this situation. During the fifteen days of its sessions, the Conference adopted a considerable number of resolutions, for the most part unanimously.

The first series of resolutions referred to conditions of labour in the mines. It was resolved that the age limit for the admission of children to employment in mines should be twelve years in Southern countries and fourteen years in others, and that women should be excluded from work in mines entirely. It was further resolved to guarantee as far as possible the health and safety of miners and an adequate State inspection of mines, to certify as mining engineers only men of experience and duly attested competence, to render relations between mineowners and workers as direct as possible with a view to conducing to mutual confidence and respect, and to institute measures of relief and insurance against the consequences of disease, accident, old age and death. It was recommended that in the solution of industrial disputes, voluntary direct negotiation between employers and employees should be resorted to as a general rule, with ultimate recourse, in case of necessity, to arbitration. The question of Sunday labour was also discussed. It was resolved that it was desirable to prohibit it in general, with certain specified exceptions. These exceptions related to continuous process industries involving undertakings which supply articles of prime necessity and to seasonal industries.

Further resolutions related to the protection of children. It was resolved that it was desirable that children should be excluded from industrial employment until ten years of age in Southern countries, and until twelve years of age in others. Under the age of fourteen years they should not be allowed to work at night or on Sunday, nor to exceed a limit of six hours of daily work broken by a rest period of at least half an hour, nor to be admitted to unhealthy or dangerous occupations, unless in exceptional cases where special protection was provided.

While on paper these resolutions appeared to have considerable importance, in reality the Conference was a failure. The resolutions in fact amounted simply to abstract propositions of what was considered to be desirable. They were not conventions to which the States, whose representatives voted for them, envisaged any immediate prospect of giving application in their own national legislation. This feature distinguishes the Conference of Berlin from the Conferences of the International Labour Organisation. At International Labour Conferences the Draft Conventions which are adopted are voted for by Government representatives on the full understanding that their Governments intend, in authorising them to vote, to introduce national legislation at the earliest possible moment to give effect to the provisions contained in the Draft Conventions and Recommendations. As a result of the Berlin Conference, no measures were taken by any State to give immediate application to the pious resolutions which were there adopted. The Berlin Conference, however, although its immediate results were nil, constitutes a landmark of the first importance in the history of international labour legislation. It was the first occasion on which accredited official delegates of States had come together to discuss questions of labour legislation.

Between the meeting of the Berlin Conference in 1890 and the First Session of the International Labour Conference in 1919, the ideal of international labour legislation was gradually brought nearer to practical realisation by two series of efforts. On the one hand, the International Association for Labour Legislation was created, and through its conferences, led to the first really effective steps in international labour legislation. On the other hand, various international workers' conferences, both of a trade union and of a political variety, kept before the minds of the workers the importance of the international solution of labour and industrial difficulties. To a certain extent, the development which thus took place in the realisation of this ideal ran on parallel lines. The International Association for Labour Legislation and the workers' internationals consciously or unconsciously influenced one another. If more direct and concrete results were achieved by the former association, the influence of the latter group should not be overlooked, especially in its later phases.

*The International Association for Labour Legislation.*—The International Association for Labour Legislation originated as a result of a conference held at Brussels in 1897. At this Congress a certain degree of continuity with the Berlin Conference was maintained, owing to the fact that many of the delegates to the Berlin Conference were present at Brussels. Unlike, however, the Berlin Conference, Brussels was not official. It is true that some Governments sent delegates, among them Germany, Belgium and France, but for the most part the members of the Congress came as private individuals. Many men of distinction in the field of labour legislation were present. The Congress was presided over by Baron Berlepsch.

The Agenda of the Conference was in the main tentative and interrogatory in character. It asked for information concerning the development of labour legislation in the various countries subsequent to the Berlin Conference, and enquired as to the situation in the different States of industrial importance with regard to the matters dealt with in certain resolutions of that Conference. In addition, various questions were put as to the possibility or desirability of international labour protection—the regulations, if any, to be made in connection with small industry and homework ; the propriety of the concurrent adoption by all industrial States of the regulations imposed upon dangerous industries by some of them ; the proper means for ensuring the better application of protective legislation ; the establishment of international relations between the Labour Departments in various States ; and the compilation of international labour statistics through the creation of an international labour bureau.

The Congress was content for the most part to exchange views with regard to the questions on the Agenda. There appeared to be a possibility that it would be decided to establish an international labour bureau, for it was universally admitted that such a bureau would be desirable. The Congress, however, failed to agree in deciding to advocate it owing to a divergence of opinion as to the workability of such an office unless it were a private bureau.

Another matter to which special attention was devoted by the Congress was the question of the abolition of the use of industrial poisons by international agreement, and the view was expressed that the first attempts with a view to such legislation might be made in the domain of the international prohibition of the use of white lead and the use of white phosphorus.

The Brussels Congress, however, deserves its place in history for what took place immediately after rather than for any decision reached by the Congress itself. After the adjournment of the Conference a Committee of three, consisting of Professor Mahaim, Duke Ursel and Mr. Brants, was formed to function as a Continuation Committee. This Committee undertook to attempt to prepare the way for the establishment of an international labour association representative of all the parties interested in the legal protection of labour. The Committee drafted the constitution of such an association, and a further step in advance was secured when a Labour Section in France was organised and summoned those interested to another International Labour Congress, which was held in Paris in 1900.

The Paris Congress, which met from July 25 to 29, 1900, was attended by official delegates of Holland, Russia, Austria, Belgium, the United States and Mexico,[1] while many other countries were represented non-officially by prominent men and women. The Congress devoted its attention to the consideration of four questions—the legal limitation of the length of the working day ; the prohibition of night work ; factory inspection ; and finally, the formation of a union or an international association for the legal protection of labour. This Congress, like the others, contented itself with discussion rather than with decisions leading to immediately realisable action.

It was the general opinion of the Conference that the consensus of opinion of past congresses seemed to favour a period of eleven hours of work per day, to be gradually reduced to ten. It severely condemned night work, and factory inspection was considered to be an essential institution capable of further development in well-defined respects. The real importance of the Congress, however, lay in its definite decision to establish an international association. The Conference considered that the creation of an official international office was undesirable, owing to the complications that would probably ensue between this office and the member States. It was therefore decided to organise an unofficial office under the International

[1] It is an odd instance of the topsy-turvydom of history that of these six States three are the only States of any importance which to-day do not form part of the International Labour Organisation.

Association for Labour Legislation, which was then definitely established.

The work of laying the foundations of the organisation of the new Association was entrusted to a committee of six : M. Scherrer (Switzerland), Baron Berlepsch (Germany), M. Cauwès (France), Dr. Phillippovich (Austria), Dr. Toniolo (Italy) and Prof. Mahaim (Belgium). The Association was to be directed by a bureau chosen by the committee of delegates representing the various national sections. These national sections were to be wholly autonomous bodies organised in accordance with the desires of the nationals concerned, each with its own programme. Financial support was derived from voluntary personal contributions and voluntary State subventions. Under the direction of the bureau, a permanent International Labour Office with a regular salaried staff was established at Basle.

The aims of the Association were summarised under the following five headings :—

1. To serve as a bond of union to all who believe in the necessity for Labour Legislation.
2. To organise an International Labour Office.
3. To facilitate the study of Labour Legislation in all countries, and to provide information on the subject.
4. To promote International Agreements on questions relating to conditions of Labour.
5. To organise International Congresses on Labour Legislation.

Its success was steady, and, in all, fifteen national sections were established, for Germany, Austria, Belgium, Denmark, Spain, America, Finland, France, Great Britain, Hungary, Italy, Norway, Holland, Sweden, Switzerland.

The First Delegates' Meeting of the International Association for Labour Legislation was held at Basle in 1901. The Conference defined the functions of the International Labour Office, indicating among the tasks of chief importance the scientific investigation and comparison of national legislative measures and the solution of the various problems involved in dangerous and unhealthy occupations, the night work of women, and the use of poisons, especially white lead and white phosphorus, in manufacturing processes. The attention of the Office was specially directed to questions of insurance against accidents and diseases, especially in their relation to foreign labour.

In the following year the Second Delegates' Meeting was held at Cologne, with an attendance of forty-four delegates representing twelve national sections. The meeting confined its work chiefly to two topics—the night work of women, and the use of white lead and white phosphorus in industry. The special interest of this Conference was its decision to submit the consideration of each of these questions to an expert commission. In this way the Conference avoided the danger of too hasty decisions on problems which were clearly seen to involve very serious technical difficulties. Thus early, therefore, the International Association for Labour Legislation laid the basis of the procedure which has since been universally adopted by the International Labour Conference.

These questions, together with others, were discussed at the Third Delegates' Meeting held at Basle in 1904. This meeting may, however, be passed over in silence, and we may immediately proceed to consider the work of the Conference of 1905, which constitutes an epoch in the history of international labour legislation.

In 1905 the two questions—the use of white phosphorus in the manufacture of matches, and the prohibition of the night work of women—which had thus received preliminary examination by the Commissions appointed by the International Association for Labour Legislation, formed the subject of the labours of a Conference held in May (8th to 17th) at Berne. Representatives of fifteen European States were present. The Conference had first to decide on its procedure. Three possibilities were considered :—

1. That definitive conventions should be concluded on the spot reserving the exchange of ratifications to Governments;
2. That tentative agreements should be drafted of a purely technical character for subsequent diplomatic revision ;
3. That resolutions of a non-binding character should be drawn up.

The second of these three courses of possible action was unanimously adopted.

The Conference appointed two committees for the examination of the two questions on its agenda. Much difficulty arose in connection with the abolition of white phosphorus. This was due, as might have been expected, to the strength of international competition in the match-making industry. Japan was not represented at the Conference, and it was recognised by all representatives of countries in which the match-making industry was of importance that any restriction of the employment of white phosphorus which was not accepted by Japan would cause serious prejudice to the trade of other countries in which this restriction had been accepted. In the end, however, an agreement was reached according to which it would become unlawful after December 31, 1910, to import, manufacture or offer for sale matches containing white phosphorus, provided all the countries represented at the meeting, and also Japan, should adhere and deposit their act of ratification by December 31, 1907.

An agreement was also reached with regard to the night work of women. It provided that the industrial night work of women should be prohibited, except in the case of enterprises employing ten or less men and women workers, and except in the case of undertakings in which only members of the same family are employed. It was provided that the period of rest should be at least eleven consecutive hours, including the interval between 10 p.m. and 5 a.m. Provision was made for the suspension of the interdiction of night work in cases of *force majeure* and certain seasonal industries.

This Conference therefore marked a stage in the evolution of international labour legislation, inasmuch as the decisions of the Conference were not mere pious resolutions, but drafts of practical labour conventions on which it was seriously intended by those present that the States which they represented should take action. In fact, in the great majority of the prominent industrial countries, the decisions reached by this first technical

Conference at Berne have been incorporated in national legislation.

In the following year these drafts of conventions which had been established by the technical experts of the various States were submitted to an International Diplomatic Conference held, again at Berne, from September 17th to 26th. The Draft Conventions as adopted by the 1905 Conference were re-drafted, but in every case the substance of the original Conventions remained. One notable addition was made, however, in the text of each Convention. This article is as follows :—

It is incumbent upon each of the contracting States to take the administrative measures necessary to ensure the strict execution of the terms of the present Convention within their respective territories.

Each Government shall communicate to the others through the diplomatic channel the laws and regulations which exist or shall hereafter come into force in their country with regard to the subject-matter of the present Convention, as well as the periodical reports on the manner in which the said laws and regulations are applied.

The insertion of this article indicates the anxiety of the signatory States each to secure as far as possible that the other States would loyally apply the Convention which they had signed. The initiative in this matter was taken by the British delegates, who also advocated the creation of an International Commission charged with superintending the execution of the provisions of the Convention. It was felt, however, by most of the delegates present that the institution of such a Commission would lead to the danger of an invasion of national sovereignty. In the end, a resolution was adopted by representatives of ten States, which provided for the institution of a commission of a purely advisory character, to which questions or disputed points might be referred, and whose duty it would be to give an opinion. The right was reserved, however, to contracting States to submit questions to arbitration in conformity with Article 16 of the Hague Convention, even if the matter had previously formed the subject of an advisory opinion of the Commission.

Only the briefest mention can be made of the Conferences held by the International Association for Labour Legislation between the Berne Conference of 1906 and the Berne Conference of 1913. Between these two large Conferences the Fourth Delegates' Meeting was held in 1906 at Geneva, the Fifth Delegates' Meeting at Lucerne in 1908, the Sixth Delegates' Meeting at Lugano in 1910, and the Seventh Delegates' Meeting at Zurich in 1912. The Lugano Conference took measures to prepare the way for a second set of two international conferences to draft international conventions prohibiting the night work of young persons entirely, and the day work of women and young persons in excess of ten hours. The delegates of Germany, Austria, Hungary, Belgium, Bulgaria, Denmark, Spain, France, Great Britain, Italy, Norway, the Netherlands, Portugal, Russia, Sweden and Switzerland duly assembled at Berne on September 15, 1913.

The same procedure as in the case of the first two Berne Conferences was followed. In other words, the 1913 Conference was a technical conference intended to be followed by a diplomatic conference in 1914. Two Draft Conventions were adopted. The first provided for the general prohibition of the night work of young persons under sixteen years of age, and absolute prohibition for all young persons under fourteen. Both of these principles were applicable to all establishments in which more than ten persons were employed. Certain exceptions were permitted.

The second Draft Convention concerned the determination of the length of the working day for workers under sixteen and for women. The Draft Convention approved by the Conference provided for a ten-hour day for these classes of workers, but with the alternative limitation of a maximum period of sixty hours per week, provided that no single working day was to exceed ten-and-a-half hours. Hours of work were to be interrupted by one or more rest periods, one of which at least was to occur immediately after the first six hours of work. In cases where work was not of more than six hours' duration, no break would be necessary.

It was intended to submit these two Draft Conventions to a Diplomatic Conference to be held in the following year. As a consequence, however, of the War, the meeting was cancelled. It was never held, for out of the War was born the new official Organisation, which for the future was to be responsible for the organisation of International Labour Conferences.

*The International Socialist and Trade Union Movement.*—No account of the development of the movement for international labour legislation would be complete if it did not devote attention to the encouragement given to this movement by the socialist and trade union internationals. The relation between the internationals and the International Labour Organisation is not by any means so close as that between the Organisation and the International Association for Labour Legislation. It would be unscientific, however, to ignore the influence exerted during the latter half of the nineteenth century on public opinion in its support of social reform by the socialist and trade union internationals; and at the end of this period, as we shall see, it was a socialist international which drafted a labour charter similar in many respects to that finally incorporated in Part XIII of the Peace Treaty.

The international labour movement may be said to have originated in a strictly historical sense in 1864, when the International Working Men's Association was formed in London with the purpose of unifying the workers of Europe and America. This Association held its first meeting at Geneva in 1866, and adopted a number of resolutions significant for the early formulation of principles which were subsequently incorporated in international conventions, and in national systems of legislation. These principles included the limitation of the duration of the standard working day and the prohibition of night work, the prohibition of the employment for wages of children between nine and thirteen years of age, the limitation of the working hours of older children, and the prohibition of night work for women and of all work injurious to health. Finally, the Association demanded that the Governments should take steps to bring about international labour protection.

Subsequent meetings of the First International were held at Lausanne, 1867, Brussels, 1868, Basle, 1869, London, 1871, and The Hague, 1872. At the last Conference a split took place in the Association, and the anarchistic element was expelled. This scission resulted in the disruption of the organisation.

The so-called Second International was constituted in the year 1889 in Paris. It was attended by four hundred delegates representing trade unions and socialist and anarchist organisations of twenty countries. The Congress adopted a programme including the prohibition of the employment of children under fourteen and in general of night work, an eight-hour day, one day of rest in seven, the establishment of an international minimum wage and health standards and the creation of systems of State-supported national and international factory inspection.

The Second International subsequently held international conferences at intervals varying from two to four years—at Brussels, 1891, Zurich, 1893, London, 1896, Paris, 1900, Amsterdam, 1904, Stuttgart, 1907, Copenhagen, 1910, Basle, 1912. At the Paris Congress of 1900 an important event took place in the creation of a permanent organisation in order to act as a bond between the various international conferences. This newly constituted International Socialist Bureau was established at Brussels, with M. E. Vandervelde as Chairman and M. Camille Huysmans as Secretary.

Special mention should also be made of the Congresses of the International Federation of Trade Unions. This organisation, representing exclusively the trade union side of the labour movement as distinct

3

from the political side, was organised in 1898, and met regularly in various towns. Its conferences were concerned with practical detailed plans for the improvement of working conditions rather than with the semitheoretical matters which tended in later years to engage the attention of the Socialist or Second International.

These two internationals, the Socialist and the Federation of Trade Unions, were both in their own provinces progressing, and both had planned the usual conferences when the War crashed with sudden decisive intervention on the spirit of internationalism. But the spirit of international socialism was scotched, not killed, and before the end of the War socialist conferences were held which exerted a real influence on the movement for the establishment of the International Labour Organisation. Strangely enough, the initiative in this matter was taken by the American Federation of Labor, which in 1914 passed a resolution proposing the convocation of an International Labour Conference with the representatives of organised labour of the different countries to meet at the same time and place as the Peace Congress. Copics of this resolution were sent to the International Federation of Trade Unions as well as to the national trade unions in various countries. On May 1, 1916, this proposal resulted in a request to the Allied Supreme Council to consider the holding of an International Labour Conference. A Commission was appointed and authority was given to prepare for an international labour conference to be held in Leeds. The Commission consisted of the labour leaders of Great Britain, France, Italy and Belgium.

An important feature of the Leeds Conference, which met in July 1916, was a resolution which was adopted and subsequently circulated not only among the Allies, but also among the Central Powers. This resolution declared that the peace terms should ensure to the workers a minimum of guarantees of a moral as well as of a material kind concerning emigration, social insurance, hours of labour, hygiene and the protection of labour. The resolution further urged the creation of an international commission for the supervision of legislation on social insurance, labour migration, hours of work and safety. It also requested the establishment of an international labour office for the co-ordination of the labour statistics of various countries, for the creation of uniform methods of statistics and for the publication of the material then collected.

Another gathering which exercised a considerable influence upon the subsequent development of the international labour situation was organised under the auspices of the Swiss Federation of Labour and met at Berne in 1917. Delegates from the Neutrals and the Central Powers, including representatives of the national organisations of Germany, Austria, Hungary, Bohemia, Bulgaria, Denmark, Norway, Sweden, the Netherlands and Switzerland, participated in the discussions. One of the demands of this Conference was that the International Association for Labour Legislation should be explicitly recognised in the Peace Treaty as the medium for the promotion and enforcement of international protective labour legislation.

Most important of all from the point of view of its influence on the establishment of the International Labour Organisation was the International Socialist Conference held at Berne in February (2nd to 9th) 1919. Some ninety delegates representing twenty-five countries of the world were present. The great interest of this Conference from the point of view of international labour legislation was the detailed programme for a Labour Charter. This included an eight-hour day, a weekly rest period of thirty-six consecutive hours, the prohibition of female night labour, a six-hour day for children between sixteen and eighteen years of age, a system of social insurance, freedom of association, a system of employment bureaux, and " the creation of a permanent Commission for the application of international labour legislation."

This Charter undoubtedly exercised a direct influence on Article 427 of the Peace Treaty.

At the end of a century of endeavour the International Labour Organisation now is. Is it to be regarded, with Thucydides, as the *dénouement* in the unfolding of a mighty drama of the fates, or with Hegel, as the final self-externalisation of the spirit of social progress, or with the materialistic school of history, as a blind event in a sequence of blind events? Whether as dramatic climax, as philosophic culmination, or as materialistic resultant, the real significance of the International Labour Organisation is not to be the end of a sequence but the beginning of a new process. It was as a new beginning in a new world that the International Labour Organisation was intended to function. But has the new world been born?

# CHAPTER III

## THE CONSTITUTION OF THE INTERNATIONAL LABOUR ORGANISATION

THE constitution of the International Labour Organi-sation, as incorporated in Part XIII of the Peace Treaty, was drafted in Paris by the Commission on International Labour Legislation. The appointment of this Commission was one of the first acts of the Peace Conference. It was established on January 31, 1919, with the following terms of reference :—

That a Commission, composed of two representatives apiece from the five Great Powers, and five representatives to be elected by the other Powers represented at the Peace Conference, be appointed to enquire into the conditions of employment from the international aspect, and to consider the international means necessary to secure common action on matters affecting con-ditions of employment, and to recommend the form of a permanent agency to continue such enquiry and consideration in co-operation with and under the direction of the League of Nations.

The Commission elected as its President Mr. Samuel Gompers, President of the American Federation of Labor, and as its Vice-Presidents the Rt. Hon. G. N. Barnes, M.P. (British Empire), and M. Colliard (France). Its General Secretary was M. Arthur Fontaine (France), and its Assistant General Secretary Mr. H. B. Butler (British Empire).[1]

The Commission held thirty-five meetings, and on

[1] The Commission was composed as follows :—
UNITED STATES OF AMERICA: Mr. Samuel Gompers, President of the American Federation of Labor ; Hon. A. N. Hurley, President of the American Shipping Board.
THE BRITISH EMPIRE : The Rt. Hon. G. N. Barnes, M.P., Member of the War Cabinet ; Sir Malcolm Delevingne, K.C.B., Assistant Under Secretary of State, Home Office.

April 11, 1919, its Report was received by a Plenary Session of the Peace Conference, which authorised its incorporation as Part XIII of the Treaty. The International Labour Organisation was thus the direct result of the labours of the Commission on International Labour Legislation.

A brief outline must now be given of the Constitution of the Organisation as established by Part XIII of the Treaty. In the first part of the chapter only the bare bones will be displayed, to enable the reader to enjoy the advantages of an X-ray photograph without putting him to the trouble of taking it. In the second part, attention will be drawn to some of the more interesting questions to which the discussion of these provisions gave rise in the Commission on International Labour Legislation.

The objects for which the International Labour Organisation was called into being are set forth in the Preamble to the Charter of this Organisation, which is contained in Part XIII of the Peace Treaty. The text of this Preamble is as follows :—

Whereas the League of Nations has for its object the establishment of universal peace, and such a peace can be established only if it is based upon social justice :

And whereas conditions of labour exist involving such injustice, hardship and privation to large numbers of people as to produce unrest so great that the peace and harmony of the world are

---

FRANCE : M. Colliard, Minister of Labour ; M. Loucheur, Minister of Industrial Reconstruction.

ITALY : Baron Mayor des Planchés, Hon. Ambassador, Commissioner-General for Emigration ; M. Cabrini, Deputy, Vice-President of the Supreme Labour Council.

JAPAN : M. Otchiai, Envoy Extraordinary, Minister Plenipotentiary, of His Majesty The Emperor of Japan at The Hague ; M. Oka, formerly Director of Commercial and Industrial Affairs at the Ministry of Agriculture and Commerce.

BELGIUM : M. Vandervelde, Minister of Justice and of State ; M. Mahaim, Professor at Liège University, Secretary to the Belgian Section of the Association for the Legal Protection of Workmen.

CUBA : M. De Bustamante, Professor at Havana University.

POLAND : Count Zoltowski, Member of the Polish National Committee, afterwards replaced by M. Stanislas Patek, Counsellor of the Court of Cassation.

CZECHOSLOVAK REPUBLIC : M. Benés, Minister for Foreign Affairs, afterwards replaced by M. Rudolph Broz.

imperilled : and an improvement of those conditions is urgently required : as, for example, by the regulation of the hours of work, including the establishment of a maximum working day and week, the regulation of the labour supply, the prevention of unemployment, the provision of an adequate living wage, the protection of the worker against sickness, disease and injury arising out of his employment, the protection of children, young persons and women, provision for old age and injury, protection of the interests of workers when employed in countries other than their own, recognition of the principle of freedom of association, the organisation of vocational and technical education and other measures :

Whereas also the failure of any nation to adopt humane conditions of labour is an obstacle in the way of other nations which desire to improve the conditions in their own countries :

The High Contracting Parties, moved by sentiments of justice and humanity as well as by the desire to secure the permanent peace of the world, agree to the following :—

(Here follow the detailed provisions for the establishment of the International Labour Organisation.)[1]

## It was provided in Part XIII of the Treaty that the original States Members of the League of Nations

[1] The general principles that should guide the Organisation were also laid down in Part XIII of the Peace Treaty, in what has come to be known popularly as the Labour Charter. This Labour Charter is as follows :

### GENERAL PRINCIPLES.

#### Article 427.

The High Contracting Parties, recognising that the well-being, physical, moral and intellectual, of industrial wage-earners is of supreme international importance, have framed, in order to further this great end, the permanent machinery provided for in Section I, and associated with that of the League of Nations.

They recognise that differences of climate, habits and customs, of economic opportunity and industrial tradition make strict uniformity in the conditions of labour difficult of immediate attainment. But, holding as they do that labour should not be regarded merely as an article of commerce, they think that there are methods and principles for regulating labour conditions which all industrial communities should endeavour to apply, so far as their special circumstances will permit.

Among these methods and principles, the following seem to the High Contracting Parties to be of special and urgent importance :—

*First.*—The guiding principle above enunciated that labour should not be regarded merely as a commodity or article of commerce.

*Second.*—The right of association for all lawful purposes by the employed as well as by the employers.

*Third.*—The payment to the employed of a wage adequate to maintain a reasonable standard of life as this is understood in their time and country.

*Fourth.*—The adoption of an eight-hours day or a forty-eight hours week as the standard to be aimed at where it has not already been attained. [*Note continued on next page.*]

should be the original Members of this Organisation. The number of States Members has been increased since the establishment of the Organisation by new accessions, and the total number of States Members of the Organisation is now fifty-seven.

The permanent Organisation consists of—

The General Conference of representatives of the members;

The International Labour Office.

The functions of the Conference are legislative in character, those of the Office are administrative and executive.

## GENERAL CONFERENCE.

The meetings of the General Conference of Representatives of the States Members may, by Article 389 of the Treaty, be held from time to time as occasion may require, and must be held at least once in every year.

The Conference is composed of four Representatives of each of the States Members, of whom two are Government Delegates, and the two others Delegates representing respectively the employers and the workers of each of the States Members. Each Delegate may be accompanied by Advisers, who may not exceed two in number for each item on the Agenda of the Meeting.

---

*Fifth.*—The adoption of a weekly rest of at least twenty-four hours, which should include Sunday wherever practicable.

*Sixth.*—The abolition of child labour and the imposition of such limitations on the labour of young persons as shall permit the continuation of their education and assure their proper physical development.

*Seventh.*—The principle that men and women should receive equal remuneration for work of equal value.

*Eighth.*—The standard set by law in each country with respect to the conditions of labour should have due regard to the equitable economic treatment of all workers lawfully resident therein.

*Ninth.*—Each State should make provision for a system of inspection in which women should take part, in order to ensure the enforcement of the laws and regulations for the protection of the employed.

Without claiming that these methods and principles are either complete or final, the High Contracting Parties are of opinion that they are well fitted to guide the policy of the League of Nations, and that, if adopted by the industrial communities who are Members of the League, and safeguarded in practice by an adequate system of such inspection, they will confer lasting benefits upon the wage-earners of the world.

When questions especially affecting women are to be considered by the Conference, it is provided that one at least of the advisers should be a woman. These advisers may, under certain conditions, replace the Delegates at the Conference and exercise the full rights of membership. They may also act for the Delegates on Commissions and Committees set up by the Conference.

The States Members undertake to nominate non-Government delegates and advisers chosen in accordance with the industrial organisations, if such organisations exist, which are most representative of employers or workers as the case may be, in their respective countries.

The decisions of the Conference take the form either of Draft Conventions or of Recommendations. Both require for final adoption a majority of two-thirds of the votes cast. On any matter a valid vote requires the participation of at least half the delegates attending the Conference.

By Article 405 of the Treaty,

each of the Members undertakes that it will, within the period of one year at most from the closing of the session of the Conference, or if it is impossible owing to exceptional circumstances to do so within the period of one year, then at the earliest practicable moment and in no case later than eighteen months from the closing of the session of the Conference, bring the recommendation or draft convention before the authority or authorities within whose competence the matter lies, for the enactment of legislation or other action.

It is also provided in Article 405 that in the case of a Draft Convention, the Member will, if it obtains the consent of the authority or authorities within whose competence the matter lies, communicate the formal ratification of the Convention to the Secretary-General of the League of Nations, and will take such action as may be necessary to make effective the provisions of such Convention. In the case of a Recommendation, the Members will inform the Secretary-General of the action taken. If no legislative or other action is taken to make a Recommendation effective, or if the Draft

Convention fails to obtain the consent of the authority or authorities within whose competence the matter lies, no further obligation shall rest upon the Member.

It is laid down that the provisions of Article 405 shall be interpreted in accordance with the following principle :—

In no case shall any Member be asked or required, as a result of the adoption of any Recommendation or Draft Convention by the Conference, to lessen the protection afforded by its existing legislation to the workers concerned.

Article 406 provides that any Convention ratified shall be registered by the Secretary-General of the League of Nations, but shall only be binding upon the States Members who ratify it. When a State ratifies a Convention it comes under a series of obligations. It must take the necessary legislative and administrative action to bring the provisions of the Convention into operation within its country. The responsibility for securing the effective observance of the Convention by all parties within its jurisdiction rests upon the Government.

The due fulfilment by each Government of this responsibility is intended to be secured by a system of sanctions. This system is as follows :—

The initiative in lodging a complaint against any Government on the ground of non-fulfilment of its obligations, may be taken by any of the parties who can be supposed to have an interest in the matter. Any other Government which has accepted the obligation about which the complaint arises, any industrial organisation of employers or workpeople, any delegate to the Conference (and by such a channel, presumably, any industrial organisation in another country than that in which the offence is alleged), has the right to bring before the International Labour Office any case in which it is believed that a Government has failed to observe its undertakings. Moreover, since each Government is bound to make an annual report to the Office, in a form prescribed by the Governing Body of the Office, as to the measures which it has taken to secure compliance with the provisions of duly ratified Conventions, the Governing Body itself may institute enquiries.

On receipt of a complaint from any of these sources (or on its own motion), the Governing Body will communicate the substance of the complaint to the Government against which the complaint has been made, and invite its observations. If no reply is received within a reasonable time, or if the reply is thought to be unsatisfactory, the Governing Body, after publishing the complaint and the reply, may request the Secretary-General of the League of Nations to appoint a Commission of Enquiry. This Commission is to be chosen from a standing panel of experts, and is to contain three members, one representing each of the constituent interests of the Conference. None of these three may belong to a State directly concerned in the complaint.

The Commission of Enquiry is bound to make full investigation of the complaint; and all the Members of the Organisation, whether parties to the dispute or not, are pledged to assist it with all the information in their possession. It has to render a decision on all matters of fact, and make recommendations as to the steps which should be taken to remove the cause of complaint. It is also charged to indicate in its report the economic measures which might appropriately be instituted against the Government in question, if it should refuse to carry out the recommendations of the Commission. The Secretary-General of the League has then to communicate the report of the Commission to the Government concerned, which must indicate within a month's time whether it accepts the recommendations contained therein. If it declines to acquiesce, it may elect to refer the whole dispute to the Permanent Court of International Justice; or, if it does not so elect, any other Member may do so.

This Court has power to hear the whole case *de novo,* and to deal with the findings of the Commission of Enquiry as it may see fit. But its report is final. The report must contain recommendations as to the action necessary to meet the complaint, and as to the economic measures appropriate in case of default. If, in the end, the Government concerned still refuses to carry out the recommendations of the Commission, or of the Court, any other Member of the Organisation is free to take against it the measures indicated in the report. These measures may remain in force until the defaulting Government informs the Governing Body of the Office that it has taken the necessary remedial action, and its statement has been confirmed by a procedure similar to that adopted to pronounce on the justice of the complaint.

Five sessions of the Conference have now been held : the first at Washington in October–November 1919, at which six Draft Conventions and six Recommendations were adopted; the second at Genoa in June–July 1920, at which three Draft Conventions and four Recommendations were adopted; the third at Geneva in October–November 1921, at which seven Draft Conventions and eight Recommendations were adopted; and the fourth and fifth at Geneva in October 1922 and October 1923, at each of which one Recommendation was adopted. Details with regard to the decisions of these Conferences will be given in subsequent chapters.

### THE INTERNATIONAL LABOUR OFFICE.

It is provided by Article 393 that—

The International Labour Office shall be under the control of a Governing Body consisting of twenty-four persons, appointed in accordance with the following provisions.

The Governing Body of the International Labour Office shall be constituted as follows :—

Twelve persons representing the Governments ;

Six persons elected by the Delegates to the Conference representing the employers ;

Six persons elected by the Delegates to the Conference representing the workers.

Of the twelve persons representing the Governments eight shall be nominated by the Members which are of the chief industrial importance, and four shall be nominated by the Members selected for the purpose by the Government Delegates to the Conference, excluding the Delegates of the eight Members mentioned above.

The seats allotted to the eight Members which are of the chief industrial importance are at present occupied by the representatives of Belgium, Canada, France, Germany, Great Britain, India, Italy and Japan.

At present the States represented on the Governing Body are as follows :—

### GOVERNMENT REPRESENTATIVES.

| | | |
|---|---|---|
| Belgium | France | Italy |
| Canada | Germany | Japan |
| Chile | Great Britain | Poland |
| Finland | India | Spain |

### EMPLOYERS' REPRESENTATIVES.

| | | |
|---|---|---|
| Belgium | France | Italy |
| Czechoslovakia | Great Britain | South Africa |

### WORKERS' REPRESENTATIVES.

| | | |
|---|---|---|
| Canada | Germany | Netherlands |
| France | Great Britain | Sweden |

The members of the Governing Body hold office for three years. As the first appointments were made at the 1919 Conference, it fell to the 1922 Conference to make new nominations. From its establishment up to January 1, 1924, the Governing Body has held twenty sessions. Two Committees have been set up, one for finance and one upon standing orders. The Finance Committee examines the expenditure of the Office, and various questions of procedure are referred to the Committee on Standing Orders.

The duties of the Office are defined as follows in Article 396 of the Treaty :—

The functions of the International Labour Office shall include the collection and distribution of information on all subjects relating to the international adjustment of conditions of industrial life and labour, and particularly the examination of subjects which it is proposed to bring before the Conference with a view to the conclusion of international conventions, and the conduct of such special investigations as may be ordered by the Conference.

It will prepare the agenda for the meetings of the Conference.

It will carry out the duties required of it by the provisions of this Part of the present Treaty in connection with international disputes.

It will edit and publish in French and English, and in such other languages as the Governing Body may think desirable, a periodical paper dealing with problems of industry and employment of international interest.

Generally, in addition to the functions set out in this Article, it shall have such other powers and duties as may be assigned to it by the Conference.

The Treaty further provides that the Governing Body shall appoint a Director of the International Labour Office who, subject to the instructions of the Governing Body, shall be responsible for the efficient conduct of the Office and for such other duties as may be assigned to him, and shall appoint the staff, selecting persons of different nationalities so far as is possible with due regard to the efficiency of the work of the Office. A certain number of the staff appointed are to be women.

The organisation of the Office at present includes the Directorate and three Divisions, an Administrative Section and a Publications Section.

The Director of the Office is M. Albert Thomas, and the Deputy-Director Mr. H. B. Butler, C.B.

*Diplomatic Division.*—The Diplomatic Division is responsible for correspondence arising out of the general application and interpretation of Part XIII of the Treaty, for the preparation of sessions of the Conference and for the secretarial duties of the Conference and of the Governing Body; also for correspondence connected with the procedure of ratification and the application or interpretation of Draft Conventions.

*The Research Division* is responsible, as its name indicates, for the research work of the Office. The scope of its work is sufficiently indicated by the titles of the various Sections which compose it. These are as follows :—

> Statistical Section.
> Labour Legislation Section.
> Social Insurance and Disablement Service.
> Industrial Relations Service.
> Unemployment Service.
> Industrial Health and Safety Service.
> Agricultural Service.

The third main Division of the Office is the *Intelligence and Liaison Division*. This Division is divided into two Sections—the Section of International Relations and Information, and the Section of National Relations and Information. The first of these Sections contains groups responsible for correspondence and maintenance of relations with employers' organisations, trade unions, co-operative associations, and also with the miscellaneous international organisations interested in a greater or a less degree in problems of labour and industry. The Library also forms part of this Section. The second Section of the Division is responsible for general correspondence and relations with each of the States Members of the Organisation, with a view to keeping the Office informed with regard to the progress of industrial and labour legislation and events of current interest in the field of labour and industry in their respective countries. This Section contains representatives of nineteen different nationalities.

In addition to these three Divisions, the Office contains an Administrative Section, which is responsible for the work of all the central and material services of the Office, and a Publications Section, responsible, as its name indicates, for the editing, issuing and sale of all the publications of the Office.

In addition to the headquarters staff at Geneva, small Branch Offices have been established in six of the most important industrial countries, in order to assist the Office to follow more closely the principal movements in industry and labour in these countries. These Offices are established in London, Paris, Washington, Rome, Berlin and Tokyo. Correspondents of the Office have also been appointed in Brussels, Vienna, Budapest, Madrid, Prague and Warsaw.

Such is the Constitution of the International Labour Organisation, as finally agreed upon by the Commission on International Labour Legislation and adopted by the Peace Conference for embodiment in the Treaty as Part XIII.

Certain points would appear to call for comment,

and it will be convenient to consider them in the light of the discussions which took place in the Commission on International Labour Legislation.

1. *General Principles, or Permanent Organisation.*— Part XIII of the Peace Treaty contains two sections. In Section I the Constitution of the International Labour Organisation is laid down, in Section II the nine General Principles which have already been quoted are enunciated. Between these two Sections there is a certain difference of tendency, of attitude, which merits some comment. It is true that Part XIII as a whole, as it now stands, is perfectly self-consistent. Section I establishes an Organisation, and Section II lays down certain general principles for the guidance of the work of that Organisation. But the difference of tendency to which allusion has been made appeared in a much sharper form in the Commission on International Labour Legislation. On that Commission two clearly differentiated points of view were represented. In the first place, there was the point of view of the British Delegation, which submitted the first draft of the Constitution of the Organisation. In the opinion of the British Delegation, as explained by Mr. Barnes, the important thing was to establish a permanent organisation, not fettered by a system of definitely formulated principles, which would be able to work progressively for the betterment of industrial conditions in accordance with the changing circumstances of the time. According to this view, it was unpractical to expect that the Peace Conference should adopt and incorporate in a solemn instrument, to be valid for all time, principles to regulate conditions as rapidly changing as those in industry. It would be much more wise and much more desirable from the standpoint of all who have the welfare of the worker at heart to set up a living organism, whose constitution ensured that it should breathe the spirit of progress. Such a living organism, a dynamic centre of power, would provide for the steady if gradual development of the system of international labour legislation.

The other point of view was held and expressed by most of the other delegations. They considered that the Peace Conference should solemnly set its seal on definitely formulated principles which would constitute a Labour Charter. Most vigorous expression was given to this view by M. Jouhaux, the General Secretary of the Confédération générale du Travail. M. Jouhaux complained that if the Peace Conference confined itself to establishing the International Labour Organisation " the position to-morrow would be that of to-day and of yesterday, with the mere addition of some machinery." [1] He therefore warmly advocated the insertion in the text of the Treaty itself of definitely formulated principles assuring to all workers conditions of labour worthy of their efforts and corresponding to the importance of their function in society. This standpoint was strongly supported by Mr. Gompers, who mentioned that it was not enough to have constructed a mechanism : in the Treaty itself must be inscribed fundamental declarations on points of primary importance.

In the end, as we have seen, the Commission agreed to recommend not only the constitution of an International Labour Organisation, but also the inscription in the Treaty of a certain number of general principles. After much discussion on a panel of nineteen principles, compiled on the basis of draft Charters put forward by the French, Italian and United States Delegations and a list of five principles submitted by the British Delegation, the Commission finally agreed on nine general principles, which they recommended should be inserted in the Peace Treaty with the following introduction : —

The High Contracting Parties declare their acceptance of the following principles and engage to take all necessary steps to secure their realisation in accordance with the recommendation to be made by the International Labour Conference as to their practical application.

This introduction, as will be seen by referring to the text as finally inserted in the Treaty, was

[1] Report and Minutes of the Commission on International Labour Legislation, p. 340.

4

considerably modified in subsequent drafting. The nine principles were, however, embodied in the Treaty.

The years that have passed since these discussions in the Commission on International Labour Legislation have proved the soundness of the contention of the British Delegation. For no single practical measure has resulted from, or been influenced by, the fact that these nine general principles are incorporated in the Treaty. Some minds may perhaps experience a sentiment of theoretical satisfaction in contemplating these nine principles, but in practice they have lessened the hours of work of no child, lightened the lot of no woman and assured to no man an improvement in the conditions of his working life.

Such a list of principles, if no steps had been taken to secure their continued vitality, might have remained, like many another charter signed with high hope, merely a dead letter. But Part XIII of the Treaty of Peace set up an organisation, of which all the States of the world might be members, with an office whose duty would be to conserve the spirit of social justice and act as the dynamic mainspring of further progress.

And the Organisation, in its four short years of existence, has already shown that it is no blind automaton, no soulless machine. It is a living creature, which has already brought forth from its fruitful womb, often indeed with sore travail, a lusty brood of Conventions and Recommendations. And all of these, in turn, have within them the spirit of life, and are increasingly, as they are applied in various countries, bringing life and hope to the world's oppressed.

2. *The Representation of Groups or Interests.*—The Organisation embodies a constitutional innovation of the first importance. This is the provision that the International Labour Conference and the Governing Body of the Office should contain accredited representatives not only of Governments but also of workers and employers. At all official International Conferences previously held, Government delegates alone had been entitled to take part.

But the Constitution of the International Labour Organisation provides, as we have seen, that each of the Member States has the right to send to the Conference four delegates, two representing the Government itself, and two representing respectively the workers and employers of the country concerned. And the workers' and employers' delegates are in the fullest sense independent of, and on an equality with, the Government delegates. A Government does not have the power to appoint a man of straw to represent its workers or its employers. It must nominate its non-Government delegates in agreement with the industrial organisations which are most representative of its employers or workpeople. Further, the Treaty explicitly stipulates that at the Conference every delegate is entitled to vote individually. No Government has the right to bring pressure to bear on its non-Government delegates to vote as it dictates.

In adopting this Constitution, the Commission felt strongly that if the Conference was to be really representative of all those concerned with industry and to command their confidence, the employers and workpeople should not only themselves be represented, but should be allowed to express their views with complete frankness and freedom. The Commission was convinced that co-operation in the sphere of international industrial relations would be possible only if it were based on a real and independent representation of the State, capital and labour. While, however, the Commission was unanimous in this conviction, much difference of opinion made itself felt as to the relative numbers of the delegates representing the Governments, the employers and the workpeople respectively. The French, American, Italian and Cuban Delegations contended that each of these three parties should have equal voting power. They maintained that the working classes would never be satisfied with a representation which left the Government and the employers combined in a majority of three to their one. In other words, the proposal amounted to giving the States a veto on the

proceedings of the Conference which would create so
much distrust of it among the workers that its influence
would be seriously prejudiced from the start. This view
was contested by the British, Belgian and other Delegations, who pointed out that as the Conference was
not simply an assembly for the purpose of passing
resolutions, but would draw up draft conventions which
the States would have to present to their legislative
authorities, it was essential that the Governments should
have at least an equal voice. Otherwise, it might often
happen that conventions adopted by a two-thirds
majority of the Conference would be rejected by the
legislatures of the various States, which would have the
effect of rendering the proceedings of the Conference
nugatory and would quickly destroy its influence and
prestige. The adoption of a proposal to which the
majority of the Governments were opposed would not
lead to any practical result, as the legislative authorities
of the Governments whose delegates were in the minority
would in all probability refuse to accept it. Moreover,
it was likely, especially in the future, that the Government delegates would vote more often with the workers
than against them. If this were so, it was obviously
to the advantage of the latter that the Governments
should have two votes instead of one, as it would render
it easier for them to obtain a two-thirds majority, which
under the Franco-American proposal would be practically impossible, if the employers voted in a body against
them.

The Commission finally decided by a narrow majority
to maintain the proposal that each Government should
have two delegates.

Here also experience has demonstrated the wisdom
of the decision of the Commission. The hesitancy that
has been shown by Governments, even under the Constitution as it stands, in ratifying the Draft Conventions
of the Conference would naturally have been greatly
increased if they had possessed only one-third of the
votes in the Conference.

3. *The Obligations of States.*—With regard to the

obligations imposed on States by the Treaty, experience has also shown that the apparently timid decision of the Conference was a wise one, and indeed the only wise one.

The original draft proposed that any Draft Convention adopted by the Conference by a two-thirds majority must be ratified by every State participating, unless within one year the national legislature should have expressed its disapproval of the Draft Convention. This implied an obligation on every State to submit any Draft Convention approved by the Conference to its national legislature within one year, whether its own Government representatives had voted in favour of its adoption or not. This provision was inspired by the belief that, although the time had not yet come when anything in the nature of an international legislature, whose decisions should be binding on the different States, was possible, yet it was essential for the progress of international labour legislation to require the Governments to give their national legislatures the opportunity of expressing their opinion on the measures favoured by a two-thirds majority of the Labour Conference.

The French and Italian delegations, on the other hand, desired that States should be under an obligation to ratify Conventions so adopted, whether their legislative authorities approved them or not, subject to a right of appeal to the Executive Council of the League of Nations. The Council might invite the Conference to reconsider its decision, and in the event of its being reaffirmed there would be no further right of appeal.

Other delegations, though not unsympathetic to the hope that in course of time the Labour Conference might, through the growth of the spirit of internationality, acquire the powers of a truly legislative international assembly, felt that the time for such a development was not yet ripe. If an attempt were made to deprive States of a large measure of their sovereignty in regard to labour legislation, the result would be that a considerable number of States would probably resign their membership of the League of Nations rather than jeopardise their national economic position by being obliged to carry out the decisions of the International Labour Conference. The majority of the Commission therefore decided in favour of making ratification of a Convention subject to the approval of the national legislatures or other competent authorities.

The American Delegation, however, found themselves unable to accept the obligations implied in the British draft on account of the limitations imposed on the central executive and legislative powers by the constitution of certain Federal States, and notably of the United States themselves. They pointed out that the Federal Government could not accept the obligation to ratify Conventions dealing with matters within the competence of the forty-eight States of the Union, with which the power of Labour legislation for the most part rested. Further, the Federal Government could not guarantee that the constituent States, even if they passed the necessary legislation to give effect to a Convention, would put it into effective operation, nor could it provide against the possibility of such legislation being declared unconstitutional by the Supreme Judicial Authorities. The Government could not therefore engage to do something which was not within their power to perform, and the non-performance of which would render them liable to complaint.

The Commission felt that they were here faced by a serious dilemma, which threatened to make the establishment of any real system of international labour legislation impossible. On the one hand, its range and effectiveness would be seriously limited if a country of such industrial importance as the United States did not participate. On the other hand, if the scheme were so weakened as to impose no obligation on States to give effect to, or even to bring before their legislative authorities, the decisions of the Labour Conference, it was clear that its work would tend to be confined to the mere passage of resolutions instead of resulting in the promotion of social reforms with the sanction of law behind them.

The Commission spent a considerable amount of time in attempting to devise a way out of this dilemma, and ultimately succeeded in doing so. Article 19, as finally drafted, represents a solution found by a Sub-Commission consisting of representatives of the American, British and Belgian Delegations specially appointed to consider the question. It provides that the decisions of the Labour Conference may take the form either of Recommendations or of Draft Conventions. Either must be deposited with the Secretary-General of the League of Nations, and each State undertakes to bring it within one year before its competent authorities for the enactment of legislation or other action. If no legislation or other action to make a recommendation effective follows, or if a Draft Convention fails to obtain the consent of the competent authorities concerned, no further obligation rests on the State in question. In the case of a Federal State, however, whose power to enter into Conventions on labour matters is subject to limitations, its Government may treat a Draft Convention to which such limitations apply as a Recommendation only.

The Commission felt that there might in any event be instances in which the form of a Recommendation affirming a principle would be more suitable than that of a Draft Convention, which must necessarily provide for the detailed application of principles in a form which would be generally applicable by every State concerned. And experience has shown that subjects come before the Conference which, owing to their complexity, and the wide differences in the circumstances of different countries, are incapable of being reduced to any universal and uniform mode of application. In such cases a Convention is impossible, but a Recommendation of principles in more or less detail which leaves the individual States freedom to apply them in the manner best suited to their conditions undoubtedly has considerable value.

The exception in the case of Federal States is of greater importance. It places the United States and

States which are in a similar position under a less degree of obligation than other States in regard to Draft Conventions. But it will be observed that the exception extends only to those Federal States which are subject to limitations in respect of their treaty-making powers on labour matters, and further that it only extends in so far as those limitations apply in any particular case. It does not apply in the case of a Convention to which the limitations do not apply, or after any such limitations as may at present exist have been removed. Though reluctant to contemplate an arrangement under which all States would not be under identical obligations, the Commission felt that it was impossible not to recognise the constitutional difficulties which undoubtedly existed in the case of certain Federal States, and therefore proposed the above solution as the best possible in the circumstances.

The system of sanctions which may be imposed on States which do not carry out their obligations has already been explained. On one point only comment would appear to be required. The system of procedure was carefully devised in order to avoid the imposition of penalties, except in the last resort, when a State has flagrantly and persistently refused to carry out its obligations under a Convention. It was impressed on the Commission by its members, who spoke for the working classes, that in several countries the opinion of the workers was strongly in favour of the formulation of more drastic provisions in regard to penalties. The Commission, while taking the view that it would in the long run be preferable as well as more effective to rely on the pressure of international public opinion rather than on economic measures, nevertheless considered it necessary to retain the possibility of the latter in the background. If all forms of sanction were removed, the effectiveness of the scheme, and, what is almost equally important, the belief in its effectiveness, would be in a great measure destroyed.

4. *The Place of Women in the Organisation.*—A question of less intrinsic importance than any of those

which have just been discussed, but one which is full of significance for the future of the Organisation, is the part which it is destined to play for women and through women. The Commission was not allowed to overlook this matter. At its twenty-seventh meeting it received a deputation of women representing the International Women's Council, the Conference of Allied Women Suffragists, and a number of national women's organisations. The women's representatives, in addition to submitting a number of amendments to the draft of the Constitution of the International Labour Organisation, made several concrete proposals. The Conference of Allied Women Suffragists recommended that " a Female Labour Committee should be set up in every country consisting of women alone (representatives of Governments, trade union associations, scientific women, women doctors, etc.), to whom should be submitted for advice all exceptional legislative measures proposed concerning women." A very similar recommendation was made by the International Women's Council. This proposal was not adopted, but some of the detailed amendments recommended by the women's representative were adopted by the Commission and incorporated in the text of their scheme.

It should also be mentioned that two of the provisions relating to women in Part XIII owe their insertion to representations made by Miss Margaret Bondfield. These are the provisions that when questions specially affecting women are to be considered by the Conference, one at least of the advisers should be a woman, and that a certain number of members of the staff of the International Labour Office should be women.

It has seemed worth while to emphasise at this point that women had a part to play in the establishment of the Organisation. As will be seen later, they have had much to do with the carrying out of the work of the Organisation, and an extremely important part of that work has been concerned with the conditions of work of women.

5. *The Organisation and the League of Nations.*— Attention may be drawn, finally, to the fact that though little mention is made of the League of Nations in Part XIII of the Treaty, the conviction was felt by all members of the Commission that association with the League was essential not only to the existence of the Organisation, but also to the success of the League itself.    The main idea underlying the scheme embodied in Part XIII is that " the Constitution of the League of Nations will not provide a real solution of the troubles that have beset the world in the past and will not even be able to eliminate the seeds of international strife unless it provides a remedy for the industrial evils and injustices which mar the present state of society.    In proposing, therefore, to establish a permanent organisation in order to adjust labour conditions by international action, the Commission felt that it was taking an indispensable step towards the achievement of the objects of the League of Nations." [1]

Experience has shown that the association of the Organisation, as an autonomous institution, with the League of Nations, has strengthened both the Organisation and the League itself.    In the Treaty the precise nature of this association is nowhere explicitly defined. The connections between the two bodies depend on ties of common interest rather than precisely formulated constitutional bonds.    The relation has been described as that of a self-governing dominion to the mother country.    The simile is striking, but it hardly does justice to the complete autonomy of the Organisation in its relations with the Governments of the various States of the world, and on the other hand, it obscures the intimacy of the connection between the two bodies in respect of finance.

In accordance with the general principles laid down in the Treaty, a somewhat complex financial organisation has been built up to ensure unity among the institutions of the League, and at the same time to

[1] Report and Minutes of the Commission on International Labour Legislation, pp 1-2.

respect the administrative autonomy of the International Labour Office. The essential characteristics of this system are as follows : The Budget of the International Labour Organisation is prepared in draft form by the Director. The Finance Committee examines this draft and submits its proposals to the Governing Body. The draft Budget, as drawn up by the Governing Body, is submitted to the Supervisory Committee, which acts for all the institutions of the League. The Supervisory Committee makes its recommendations and, according as circumstances require, proposes reductions or increases. The Governing Body meets again and gives its opinion on the recommendations thus made. The Budget is presented to the States Members by the Secretary-General of the League of Nations, who centralises all budgetary proposals, and finally it is the Assembly which votes the Budget, after having referred it to its Fourth Commission for examination.

Thus there are direct relations between the Governing Body and the Assembly of the League. There is no intervention by the Council of the League or by the Secretariat. The fundamental autonomy of the Labour Organisation is respected. At the same time, it is laid down that four members of the Governing Body have the right to present the Budget to the Supervisory Committee, and to defend the Governing Body's proposals, and that, if necessary, a representative of the Organisation appointed by the Governing Body may defend the estimates of the Organisation before the Assembly. Thus, the gulf which might exist between the autonomous Labour Organisation and the General Assembly of Members of the League is bridged.

This machinery, although delicately adjusted, does not completely exclude certain possible complications. It is the Assembly of the League which possesses complete power in regard to finance. It is the Assembly which votes the credits necessary for the functioning of all the institutions of the League. It is the Assembly which fixes the contributions of each State and which has the right to control expenditure. If, however, the

Assembly decided to reduce certain credits and thus to suppress parts of the work of the Office undertaken by resolution of the Governing Body or by decision of the Conference, the autonomy of the Organisation would be affected, for the Governing Body has the right to lay down the policy of the Office and the Conference may also entrust the Office with any task it considers desirable. If, therefore, the Assembly of the League, in suppressing or reducing the credits of the Organisation, should infringe upon the authority of the Governing Body or of the Conference, a difficult situation would arise. Such a situation is, however, largely theoretical.

In the International Labour Conference and on the Governing Body, the Government delegates, generally speaking, control a majority. Now, these delegates receive instructions from their Governments, and these instructions cannot differ from those given to the representatives of the same Governments at the Assembly of the League. It is certain, therefore, that the general policy of the Council and Assembly of the League, and of the Governing Body and Conference of the International Labour Organisation, cannot greatly vary.

The contributions made by the various States to the expenses of the League are calculated on a system which classifies States into seven categories. The determination as to the category into which a State should go is based, in general, on the principle of capacity to pay. The coefficients of the various categories range from 1 to 88. The British Empire, excluding self-governing Dominions, pays 88 units, and such countries as Albania 1 unit. For the year 1924 the estimated Budget of the Office amounts to about 7,000,000 Swiss francs, or about £280,000. It would be difficult to discover even a second- or third-rate British Ministry which costs so little.

The relations between the League and the Organisation are not confined to this cash nexus. Arrangements have been made that a copy of the Agenda of each meeting of the Council of the League should be communicated to the Director at the same time as it is communicated to the Members of the Council, and that the Director should inform the Secretary-General as to the questions which might concern the Office. The Council would then decide as to whether the Director would be heard. This method of liaison between the Governing Body of the Office and the Council of the League has been in regular operation and has worked extremely well.

Efficient collaboration between the League and the Office has also been established in each of the aspects of their daily work where co-operation seems necessary.

The Office has been represented on all Commissions of the League of Nations whose work is in any way connected with the questions entrusted to the Office by Part XIII of the Treaty of Peace. Similarly, the League of Nations has been represented on the Commissions set up by the Governing Body in cases where the work of the Commissions is likely to interest the League.

This collaboration, thanks to a strict division of labour according to the respective competence of the two institutions, has always given the best results. This has been particularly evident in regard to questions concerning intellectual work, disablement, health, the white slave traffic, transit, mandates and Russian refugees.

# CHAPTER IV

## THE WASHINGTON CONFERENCE

THE first Session of the International Labour Conference was opened at Washington, in accordance with
the terms of the Treaty of Peace, on October 29, 1919.
The Conference thus began before the League of
Nations had been formally constituted, and the International Labour Organisation accordingly had the
honour of being the first of the system of international legislative, administrative and judicial institutions provided for by the Peace Treaty to come into
effective operation. That the first international body
to commence its activities was concerned not with
political questions, but with problems of industry, is of
peculiar significance. International relations were not
henceforth to be the prerogative of official diplomats.
They were to be dealt with by the people immediately
concerned, employers and workers and Government
technical experts, and were to extend to the regulation
of the conditions in which the ordinary citizens of the
world work and live.

The four years that have passed since the Washington
Conference render it possible to view its work in a
proper perspective and to form an estimate of its
enduring importance with some assurance that the
justice of that estimate will not be seriously challenged
by the future.

In this chapter an attempt will therefore be made not
only to give an account in some detail of the proceedings of the Conference, but also to estimate its ultimate
place in the history of international industrial co-operation. The Washington Conference will be treated in

greater detail than succeeding conferences, partly because it was the first of the series, partly because the problems which it faced were typical of those with which the labour conferences have had to deal, but more especially because it was, by reason of the significance of the subjects discussed and the decisions reached, the most important of all the series of the International Labour Conferences that have so far been held.

The circumstances in which the Conference met were, indeed, singularly unfavourable. Washington had been named in the Peace Treaty as the meeting-place of the first Conference partly as a compliment to President Wilson and partly in order that this first experiment in practical internationalism should have the support and prestige that close personal association with him would give to it. Unfortunately, the President had fallen seriously ill and the news that he would be unable to assist in the deliberations struck a chill to the very heart of the Conference.

Further, the general atmosphere in Washington was, if not actively hostile, at least indifferent. The United States had not ratified the Peace Treaty. The long debate in the Senate reached its climax during the sitting of the Conference and culminated in the refusal to ratify the Treaty. The Labour Part of the Treaty, establishing the International Labour Organisation, was singled out for especially bitter criticism. To a certain extent this opposition to the Treaty had its repercussion on the attitude of the public in America towards the Conference. One senator, indeed, protested strongly against the holding of the Conference in Washington at all, and even suggested the wholesale deportation of these alien agitators ! But more difficult for the Conference to bear than this open hostility was the indifference and scepticism with which the whole great adventure appeared to be generally regarded in the United States. The Conference passed a resolution inviting American employers and workers to send representatives to take part informally in the proceedings. But apart from a single visit of

Mr. Gompers, no representative came, and extraordinarily little public interest of any kind was shown in the Conference.

And there was a further difficulty which caused some concern to the more constitutionally minded delegates. Strictly speaking, the Conference had no legal status. For the Treaty, under whose auspices the Conference met, had not at that time been ratified, nor, as had already been indicated, had the League of Nations been formally constituted. Any decisions it reached would therefore have to be subsequently legitimated. This curious situation was regularised by an ingenious device. It was decided that when the Conference held its last sitting on November 29, it should not be formally closed, but merely adjourned *sine die*, with power to the newly constituted Governing Body of the Office to summon it again or to take such other action as was legally necessary to validate its decisions. And on January 27, 1920, at a meeting of the Governing Body in Paris, a declaration was carried formally closing the Conference. In the meantime, on January 10, 1920, the Treaty had been ratified and the League of Nations formally constituted.

It may fairly be said, then, that the circumstances in which the Conference met were peculiarly unhappy. And yet, as frequently happens, this unfavourable environment reacted as a powerful stimulant on the Conference. The delegates were thrown back on themselves. Internal differences, which at one time threatened to become serious, were healed, and a spirit of unity grew steadily stronger in the Conference. And it is not too much to say that the Conference was very largely indebted for its harmonious functioning and the unanimity of its decisions to its environment of scepticism and criticism. It was the trustee of the spirit of Internationalism in a country in which the word was anathema, and it felt that it had a sacred duty to show by its example that Internationalism in practice was real and living.

The Conference was attended by representatives of

39 nations. Every European country was represented, with the exception of the former enemy countries and Russia.[1] There was almost a full representation of the South American Republics, a circumstance of peculiar fitness in a conference held in the Pan-American Building. Delegates were present from the Extreme Orient, China, Japan and Siam; and, a fact of special interest to the British Empire, Canada, India and South Africa were represented as separate and independent units for the first time in the history of international assemblies.

Altogether 123 delegates were present at the meeting, of whom 73 were Government delegates, 25 employers and 25 workers, and they were assisted by a body of technical advisers about 150 in number, of whom 23 were women.

The Conference was significant not only because of the number of the delegates, but also on account of their diversity. They differed, of course, in race, in tongue, in colour and in temperament. They differed also in the interests they represented. Governments had sent Cabinet Ministers, Ambassadors, civil servants, technical experts, and from all parts of the globe great captains of industry and well-known trade union leaders had come to give expression to their points of view.

In each of the Conferences of the Organisation there has been some material feature to strike the eye, if

---

[1] On the second day of the Conference, it was decided to admit Germany and Austria into the International Labour Organisation. The reasons in favour of this decision were strongly expressed by M. Jouhaux, the Secretary-General of the C.G.T., who pointed out that to admit the enemy countries was not only in the spirit of the League of Nations, upon which the reconstruction of the world so largely depended, but was also practically necessary, since without their co-operation no system of international labour legislation could be really effective in Europe. This view was adopted by the Conference by a majority of 71 to 1. Both the German and the Austrian Governments accepted the invitation, but owing to transport difficulties they were unable to sail in time to reach Washington before the close of the Conference.

The Conference also decided, after a debate which examined the questions of principle involved, to admit the delegation of Finland to take part in the Washington Conference, on the same conditions as other countries which had not yet adhered to the Covenant of the League of Nations. Luxemburg was subsequently admitted on the same terms.

not the imagination.  In the case of the Washington Conference, the building in which it met was peculiarly appropriate.  The Pan-American Building belongs to an organisation covering all the States of the American continent, which has as its main aim the promotion of friendly intercourse between them and the rest of the world.  A picturesque note in the hall in which the Conference met was provided by the miniatures of the national flag of each delegation which marked the place where it sat.

The organisation of the Conference is of special interest owing to its international character.  The system of organisation will therefore be explained in some considerable detail, partly because of its inherent interest and partly because the same system has been followed in the case of all successive sessions of the Conference.

Before passing to this, however, it will be well to say a word with regard to the preliminary preparation of the Conference.  Much of the success which attended the organisation of the Conference itself was due to the firm foundation that had been laid by the preparatory work of the Organising Committee.  Within two days of the adoption of Part XIII of the Treaty, the Organising Committee of the Washington Conference had begun its work, and during the ensuing three months held frequent sessions in London and in Paris. The Organising Committee was composed of representatives of seven different States, under the Chairmanship of M. Arthur Fontaine, of the French Ministry of Labour, and with Mr. H. B. Butler, C.B., of the British Ministry of Labour, as Secretary.  The Organising Committee drew up a provisional scheme of standing orders, in accordance with which the whole proceedings of the Washington Conference were conducted.  It prepared questionnaires on the items of the Agenda [1]

---

[1] The full Agenda of the Conference as fixed by the Peace Treaty was as follows :—

1. Application of principle of the eight-hour day or of the forty-eight hour week.

of the Conference and it circulated them to all the Governments which had a right to participate in the Conference, inviting them to supply information with regard to the existing legislation and practice in their countries on the items in question, and also as to the attitude of the Governments towards proposals for further legislation. On the basis of the data supplied in response to these questionnaires, the Committee prepared a series of reports containing in summary form the relevant information, and also drafts of Conventions which it was proposed should serve as a basis for the discussion of the Conference. These reports were circulated to the Governments of the States which it was expected would take part in the Conference some weeks before its opening in order that the countries might have an opportunity of considering their attitude towards the proposed reforms and of instructing their delegates as to the position which they should adopt at the Conference itself.

Owing mainly to the extremely technical nature of most of the questions with which it had to deal, the Conference decided to remit these questions for examination and recommendation to Commissions. In addition, three general Commissions were appointed to facilitate the business of the Conference. The first was a Commission of Selection appointed to nominate the members of Commissions and Committees for the approval of the Conference and generally to regulate the course of its business. This Commission was constituted in the same manner as the Governing Body

---

2. Question of preventing or providing against unemployment.
3. Women's employment—
    (a) Before and after childbirth, including the question of maternity benefit.
    (b) During the night.
    (c) In unhealthy processes.
4. Employment of children :
    (a) Minimum age of employment.
    (b) During the night.
    (c) In unhealthy processes.
5. Extension and application of the International Conventions adopted at Berne in 1906 on the prohibition of night work for women employed in industry and the prohibition of the use of white phosphorus manufacture of matches.

and consisted of twelve Government members, six employers and six workers. The Chairman was M. Arthur Fontaine, of the French Ministry of Labour, and the Secretary was Mr. H. B. Butler, the Secretary-General of the Conference. The Commission of Selection was of the greatest assistance to the Conference. Owing to its constitution, it possessed a fairly complete knowledge of the interests and capacities of the delegates of the Conference and it was therefore able to nominate to the Commissions those who were best able, by reason of their special knowledge, to assist in the discussion of the point at issue and at the same time to preserve a fair balance on each Commission not only of the different constituent elements of the Conference, but also of the different nationalities or groups of nationalities represented.

In practice, the Commission of Selection became the Executive Committee of the Conference. It arranged the order of business for each session and did much to assist, by the selection and arrangement of business, to guide the general labours of the Conference as a whole.

Two general Commissions were also appointed with a more limited field of action. These were the Commission on Standing Orders, whose duty it was to revise the draft standing orders prepared by the Organising Committee with a view to future Conferences, and the Commission on Credentials, whose function it was to examine the credentials of the delegates to the Conference.

In addition to these general Commissions, the Conference appointed a Commission for each item or group of items on the Agenda. This procedure was followed with one important exception. In the case of Hours of Labour, the Conference did not at once proceed to appoint a Commission. A discussion took place in full conference on this question. It soon became clear, however, that the Conference would fail to reach an agreed conclusion if a general discussion in plenary sessions should continue on what was, in fact, the most difficult and complicated question which could have been submitted to it.  The debate became extremely confused and complications were constantly imported into the discussion which it required much time and patience to remove.  It became clear, therefore, that the experiment of asking the Conference to legislate as a whole on a question whose issues had not previously been carefully sifted in Commission was a failure. The Conference therefore decided to refer the matter to Commissions.  The experiment was useful for the Conference, as it never again attempted to legislate in full session on a technical matter without first receiving a report from a Commission.

The Commissions consisted of equal numbers of Government, employers' and workers' representatives. It will be remembered that a long discussion took place on the Commission on International Labour Legislation at the Peace Conference on the question of the proportion of the representation of the various groups, and it was finally agreed that the representation accorded to Governments should be equal to that of both workers and employers taken together.  It was felt, however, that although the Governments by the Peace Treaty had been given a double representation in the Conference and on the Governing Body, there was no reason why in the Commissions which were appointed to conduct the preliminary examination of the question, the principle of equal representation should not be adopted.  The two main arguments in favour of this arrangement were, first, that it promoted mutual confidence between the groups, and in the second place, it permitted workers and employers to express more freely and fully in Commissions their points of view than would otherwise have been the case.  At the same time, the system had the disadvantage, that owing to the necessity of limiting the size of the Commissions, a certain number of Governments which would have wished to be represented on the Commissions were necessarily excluded.  It was clear that the majority of Governments could not be represented on any particular Commission, although they had full opportunity to place any evidence which they pleased before it. In practice, the Governments not represented on a Commission which were particularly anxious that their point of view should be emphasised, either confided to a workers' or an employers' representative from their country the duty of expressing their point of view, or requested the Government representative of some country which had some connection, either racial, linguistic or geographical, with it, to give expression to its point of view. The frequency with which arrangements of this kind were made illustrated the extent to which mutual confidence and harmonious co-operation were found possible in this first Conference.

The Commissions worked extremely hard. All of them sat continuously for more than a week, some of them met twice daily. The effect of constant association in promoting understanding and appreciation of varying points of view is clearly expressed by the Secretary-General of the Conference :—

It was interesting to notice how much close contact round a table did towards breaking down the barriers of language and nationality, and towards promoting understanding of each other's views among the members of the different groups. In some cases, and especially on the question of the hours of labour, there was a strong divergence of view between employers and workers, between whom the Government delegates acted as mediators. In other cases, however, difference of view was determined by national custom and habit of mind rather than by group interests. It was not at all uncommon to find employers siding with workers, or workers with Government delegates, on questions of principle, on which each delegate had to make up his own mind, and which did not fall within any of the usual cadres of economic theory.[1]

In all cases but one the Commissions found it possible to submit to the Conference a more or less unanimous report. In one case, a majority and a minority report were submitted. The Reports of the Commissions were considered clause by clause in full Conference. Every delegate had an opportunity of speaking, if he so

[1] Cf. *Labour as an International Problem*, edited by E. John Solano. (*The Washington Conference*, 1919, by H. B. Butler, C.B.), p. 207.

wished, on the Report. In practice, the Reports submitted by the Commissions were amended only on points of comparative detail, and then adopted as a whole by the vote of the Conference. The decisions of the Conference were then sent to the Drafting Committee, composed of legal experts, to be given proper legal form. After being worked upon by the Drafting Committee, the decision was re-submitted to the Conference either in the form of a Draft Convention or a Recommendation for final acceptance or rejection. At its final reading no debate took place. The Conference voted by roll-call on the Convention as a whole and, as it happened, in every case recorded a favourable decision by more than the prescribed statutory majority.

The secretarial work of the Conference was ensured by a staff consisting of Mr. H. B. Butler, as Secretary-General, an American and an Italian Deputy Secretary-General, and a staff of interpreters, secretaries and typists. A verbatim record of each session was taken and issued in accordance with parliamentary practice in printed form to the delegates on the following morning. These records were issued in French, English and Spanish.

The language difficulty did not present as much trouble as had been anticipated. The official languages of the Conference were English and French, and every word spoken in full Conference in English or French was translated into the other language by an interpreter. It was provided that those who were unable to speak either in English or French could speak in their own tongue provided that they supplied an interpreter competent to translate their remarks into one of the official languages. In point of fact, the only other languages in which speeches were made were Spanish, Italian and Dutch, and the number of such speeches was not great. The fact that interpretation was necessary naturally made the proceedings somewhat slow. The necessity of interpreting every remark also seriously interfered with the continuity of the discussion, and a debate which had it been conducted in one language would have followed a well-marked course, sometimes meandered bewilderingly owing to the fact that the true line of advance became confused by irrelevant suggestions which, had the proceedings been conducted in one language, would immediately have been seen to be irrelevant.

One of the greatest difficulties arising from the fact that the Conference was bi-lingual was connected with the necessity of securing absolute harmony in the final texts of the Draft Conventions and Recommendations adopted. It was provided that both the English and the French texts of the decisions should be equally authentic. In spite of the extreme care with which Conventions were drafted and the two texts compared, slight divergencies were not wholly excluded. The difficulty was due largely to the fact that representatives whose native or secondary language is English are satisfied to assure themselves that the English text is what they mean, while those for whom French is the native or secondary language are equally satisfied if the French text represents what they understand to be the decision. It is only, in general, the secretarial staff of the Conference, who do not have in mind either of the backgrounds of interpretation which the English- or the French-speaking delegates bring to the text, who really care whether the two texts conform. Under these circumstances, it is remarkable that so few divergencies have in fact later been discovered by the jurists of the various countries, in spite of the efforts that have often been made to find them.

*Hours of Work.*—The Treaty of Peace had itself laid down as one of the principles of an international industrial order the limitation of hours of work to eight per day or forty-eight per week. The Government delegates to the Conference therefore began their deliberations on this subject with their respective Governments already committed in principle to the acceptance of this limitation. But experience at the Conference and elsewhere has shown that the acceptance of a proposal in principle, and the detailed elaboration of it into a legislative scheme, are two wholly different things. The length and complexity of the debate illustrated that great differences of opinion on points of detail may continue to exist even when a principle is accepted.

The question of the regulation of hours of labour, even within a single country, presents problems of immense difficulty. It is needless to say that this difficulty is greatly increased when an attempt is made to secure regulation on an international scale. In every country where the general principle of the eight-hour day has been adopted, it has been found necessary to make exceptions and modifications to meet the peculiar requirements of different trades and industries. In view of this, some of the delegates to the Conference were inclined to think that the variety and complexity of the problems presented by the application of the eight hours principle on an international scale was such as to make a hopeful result impossible.

In spite, however, of all the difficulties which emerged in the debate, the Conference succeeded in adopting a Draft Convention, with only one dissentient vote. The Convention as adopted provides that the working hours of persons employed in any public or private industrial undertaking, or in any branch thereof other than an undertaking in which only members of the same family are employed, shall not exceed eight in a day and forty-eight in a week. Special provision is made that where by law, custom or agreement between employers' and workers' organisations, or where no such organisations exist, between workers' and employers' representatives, the hours of work on one or more days of the week are less than eight, the limit of eight hours may be exceeded on the remaining days of the week ; provided, however, that in no case shall the daily limit of eight hours be exceeded by more than one hour. Further, in the case of persons employed in shifts, it shall be permissible to employ persons in excess of eight hours in any one day and forty-eight hours in any one week if the average number of hours over a period of three weeks or less does not exceed eight hours per day and forty-eight hours per week. In the case of continuous process industries a fifty-six-hour week is permitted. A special provision was inserted providing for the regulation of overtime and stipulating that the rate of pay for overtime shall not be less than one and a quarter times the regular rate.

Such in its bare outlines is the Draft Convention on hours of labour. One or two special points in connection with the Convention, or with the discussion which led to its adoption, deserve special mention.

With regard to the principle itself, the Organising Committee had prepared a draft to serve as a basis for the discussions of the Conference which confined itself to formulating the principle of the forty-eight-hour week without dealing with the daily period of work. The workers' delegates at the Conference objected strongly to the omission of the specification of the daily period, and after discussion it was agreed that the normal day's work should be limited to eight hours, but that in cases where less than eight hours was worked on one or more days of the week, the time so lost might be made up on the remaining days provided that in no case should the day's work exceed nine hours. This means that where the weekly half-holiday is customary, the weekly period of work need not necessarily be reduced to forty-four or forty-five hours. A resolution was, however, added by the Commission to the effect that the Draft Convention should not interfere with cases in which the workers already enjoyed more favourable conditions as regards hours of work than were provided in the Draft Convention.

The principles thus agreed upon were to apply to industry in the widest sense of the term, not excluding the transport of passengers or goods by road, rail, sea, or inland waterway. As regards maritime and inland water traffic it was agreed that the practical application of the principle would have to be worked out by a special Conference. The Conference which actually dealt with this problem was the Genoa Conference held in the succeeding year.

The problem of overtime gave rise to considerable discussion. The Organising Committee had drafted a schedule of processes in which the normal limit of forty-eight hours might be extended, for example, in the case of men not engaged in continuous work throughout the day, or whose attendance before or after the normal hours is necessary for the starting or the maintenance of the plant ; and also a schedule of industries in which, owing to special conditions, overtime might be permitted provided it was limited to a maximum of one hundred and fifty hours in the year. The Commission decided, however, that it was impossible to lay down rigid rules on these matters, without the most careful preliminary investigation in all the countries affected, and they therefore adopted more elastic principles which it was hoped would still ensure that where such exceptions to the general rule might prove indispensable they should not be abused.

In the first place, they laid it down that all such exceptions should be allowed only after consultation with the organisations of employers and workers concerned. The principle of collective agreements between employers' associations and trade unions was thus given the fullest recognition and was adopted as the most practical method for the regulation of modern industrial conditions. Further, in order to make it economically disadvantageous for employers to suggest that overtime should be worked, it was provided that for all overtime worked, not less than 25 per cent. should be added to the normal rate of wages. The rate thus fixed represented a compromise between the employers' view, which was strongly opposed to any overtime rate being fixed at all, and the workers' claim that the rate should be 50 per cent. higher than the ordinary rate.

In order to ensure the proper enforcement of the Convention, provisions were added as to the steps which employers should be required to take by law in order to make known to the workers the hours of work, and the Governments were placed under the obligation to supply all the information required by the International Labour Office for the purpose of its Annual Report. The main aim of the Convention was on the one hand to lay down principles clearly and unambiguously, and, in the second place, to draft the detailed regulations on the one hand with sufficient elasticity to permit of their ready adaptation to meet varying conditions in different countries, and, on the other hand, with sufficient rigidity to ensure their equal application in all countries.

The Draft Convention also included special provisions to deal with the case of the countries in which abnormal industrial conditions exist. A special Commission had been appointed to deal with the case of special countries, and this Commission submitted a separate report to the Conference. This Commission was breaking entirely new ground. No attempt had ever been made before to bring the conditions of labour in Oriental and tropical countries into relation with those existing in Europe and North America. The special provisions for these countries may be rapidly enumerated.

In the case of Japan, it is provided that the actual working hours of persons of fifteen years of age or over in any public or private industrial undertaking shall not exceed fifty-seven in the week, except that in the raw silk industry the limit may be sixty hours in the week. In the case of miners and persons under fifteen years of age the working week is fixed at forty-eight hours. Further, the provision in Japanese factory legislation limiting its application to places employing fifteen or more persons shall be amended so that such legislation shall apply to places employing ten or more persons. A comparison of these provisions with the legislation then existing in Japan affords convincing evidence of the great advance which the Commission's work represents. At that time, the Factory Act of Japan permitted employment in factories for thirteen hours a day, including Sundays, and also allowed one hundred and twenty hours of overtime to be worked during the year.

In the case of India, it is provided that the principle of a sixty-hour week shall be adopted for all workers in the industries covered by the Indian Factory Acts, in mines, and in certain branches of railway work. The Commission reported to the Conference that the number of persons employed in India in ordinary industrial undertakings constituted but an insignificant proportion of the whole population. They thought that in the absence of fuller information about small industries, the Conference could only usefully legislate in regard to large industrial undertakings which already came within the scope of the existing Indian Factory Acts. The decision of the Conference to fix the period of weekly work at sixty hours involved a reduction from seventy-two hours.

China, Persia and Siam were definitely excepted from the provisions of the Convention, but it was provided that provisions limiting the hours of work in these countries should be considered at a future meeting of the General Conference. The reason for this decision was that the Conference did not consider that these countries were sufficiently developed from the industrial point of view to make it possible to apply the Convention to them. The Commission, however, proposed that the Chinese Government should consider the adoption of a ten-hour day, or a sixty-hour week, for adult workers in factories and of an eight-hour day or a forty-eight-hour week for persons under fifteen years of age, together with the principle of a weekly rest-day.

In the case of Greece and Roumania, delays of two or three years were agreed upon, in the case of various specified industries.

*Unemployment.*—The prevention of, and provision against, unemployment was considered in the first place by a large Commission of thirty members. That Commission divided itself into three sub-commissions, the first of which considered questions relating to the systematic observation and prevention of unemployment ; the second, questions relating to the protection of the unemployed, especially by the organisation of employment exchanges and insurance services ; and the third, questions relating to the migration of workers from one country to another. On the basis of the reports presented by these Commissions, a series of Draft Conventions and Recommendations were adopted by the Conference.

The first of these provides that States Members of the Organisation shall be under the obligation to furnish to the Office at short intervals all the available information, statistical and otherwise, concerning unemployment, including reports of measures taken or contemplated to combat unemployment. (The Conference also instructed the Office to establish an International Commission to make recommendations as to the measures by which each State can best collect information in the form most serviceable for the purposes of comparative study.) The purpose of this Draft Convention was to attempt to ensure that when the question of unemployment should be considered at future sessions of the Conference, reliable and comparable information should be available with regard to the real extent of the problem. The enquiries of the Organising Committee had shown that while many countries had information available for the examination of problems of unemployment from a national point of view, this was by no means universally the case, and further, that such statistics as were available were frequently incomparable owing to the difference in the systems on which they are based. It is an important part of the work of the International Labour Office to compare and to collate the information supplied by the various Governments in accordance with this Draft Convention, with a view to making the results obtained in one country comparable with those in other countries, and thus contributing to the attainment of solutions on an international basis.

The Draft Convention also provides for the establishment of free public employment agencies in each country, under the control of a central authority. Committees to include representatives of employers and workers shall be appointed to advise on matters concerning the carrying on of these agencies. Where both public and private free employment agencies exist, steps are to be taken to co-ordinate the operations of such agencies on a national scale. It is also provided that those States which have established systems of insurance against unemployment shall, on terms to be mutually agreed, make arrangements whereby workers belonging to one country and working in the territory of another shall be admitted to the same rates of benefit of such insurance as those which obtain for the workers belonging to the latter.

Two Recommendations were also adopted dealing with the same problem. States in which private profit-making exchanges do not exist are recommended to prohibit their institution. States in which they do exist are recommended to permit them only under licence and as soon as possible to abolish them. Further, it is recommended that the recruiting of bodies of workers in one State for employment in another should be permitted only after agreement between the countries interested and after consultation with the employers and workers in the industries concerned.

It will be seen that the Conference in adopting these Draft Conventions and Recommendations was throughout preoccupied with the international aspects of methods of dealing with unemployment, and that, further, its conclusions dealt rather with methods of alleviation than with methods of prevention.

It did not, however, entirely abstain from considering the question of the prevention of unemployment. It is true that the only decision of the Conference relating to the prevention of unemployment prescribes a purely domestic remedy. It proposes that in every State public authorities should as far as possible reserve their programmes of public works until a cyclical depression of trade is seen to be impending, so that the demand for labour should be maintained at a more nearly uniform level than would otherwise be the case. What was considered by some delegates to be a more fundamental method of preventing unemployment, and one definitely on an international basis, was proposed for the consideration of the Conference. This was the motion of M. Baldesi, the Italian workers' delegate, that in view of the tremendous crisis of unemployment which existed in many European countries, the League of Nations should be asked to study at once the question of the proper distribution of raw materials. "Broadly speaking, we have," he stated, "on the one hand, vast quantities of raw materials awaiting the work of man to convert them to profitable use, and, on the other hand, we have nations with abundant supplies of labour anxiously seeking for those same raw materials in order to make them of value to themselves and others." This question produced one of the most interesting debates which occurred during the meeting. M. Baldesi was strongly supported by the Polish Delegation, M. Ilg of Switzerland, M. Jouhaux, and others, who, from their personal experience, were in a position to realise the acuteness of the distress in Central Europe. Their argument was summed up by M. Jouhaux in the following words :—

It is not possible that the working classes in some countries should be condemned to perpetual idleness, while other countries prevent the exportation of the raw materials which are necessary to give work to the workers in countries which do not possess them. It is not possible that the privileged situation of one country should be artificially safeguarded in defiance of the general interest. . . . There cannot be any true economic equality : there cannot be any real possibility of reconstruction for the exhausted countries : there cannot be any adequate solution of the problem of unemployment unless this question has first been solved.

On the other hand, the proposal that raw materials should be controlled internationally was strongly opposed by other delegates, who maintained that it was outside the jurisdiction of the Conference to deal with the question at all. To quote Mr. Rowell, of Canada :

I say, with great respect, this Conference has no more jurisdiction over the question of the distribution of raw materials, which the delegate from Italy referred to, than it has over the question of discovering a way of navigating from the earth to the moon. It might just as well be clearly understood that the nations which have raw materials will deal with them as they believe fair and in the national interest, but they will deal with them by their own parliaments, their own legislatures, and they will not accept international regulations with reference to the control of their own property.[1]

The motion of M. Baldesi was eventually lost by the very narrow majority of forty votes to forty-three.

The last decision of the Conference relating to unemployment was a Recommendation urging each member of the Organisation, on conditions of reciprocity and upon terms to be agreed between the countries concerned, to admit the foreign workers together with their families employed within its territory to the benefit of its laws and regulations for the protection of its own workers, as well as to the right of lawful organisation as enjoyed by its own workers. It was not without considerable debate that the Conference finally agreed on this Recommendation. The Commission had proposed it in the form of a Draft Convention. Very little objection was felt to the principle of reciprocity as such. Countries of immigration, however, felt doubts as to the practicability in all cases of carrying out such a principle. In the end, therefore, the Conference decided not to embody the principle in the rigid form of a Convention, but to give it the more elastic expression of a Recommendation.

*The Employment of Women.*—With regard to the employment of women, two important Draft Conventions were adopted. One of these prohibited the employment during the night of women in any public or private industrial undertaking. The term "night" was defined to signify a period of eleven consecutive hours including the interval between 10 p.m. and 5 a.m. This Convention was based on the Berne Convention of 1906, which prohibited the employment of women between 10 p.m.

[1] Cf. *Labour as an International Problem.* Solano, pp. 225-226.

and 5 a.m. The Berne Convention, however, had
limited the application of the prohibition to establishments in which at least ten persons were engaged. The
Commission withdrew that limitation because experience
had shown that often the worst offenders were the small
establishments which had hitherto been excepted.
Amendments to the Convention were moved by
M. Baldesi and by M. Guérin, the French employers'
delegate—the first to extend the hours of rest to 6 a.m.,
the second permitting women to be employed between
the hours of 4 a.m. and 10 p.m., or 5 a.m. and 11 p.m.
where two shifts were worked. Both these proposals,
however, were defeated. Certain special provisions were
inserted in the Convention to apply to Oriental
countries. No modifications were requested by the
Japanese representatives. In the case of India, however,
a special clause was inserted providing for the suspension of the application of the Convention in any
industrial undertaking except factories as defined by
the national law.

The second Draft Convention relating to the employment of women provides that in any public or private
industrial or commercial undertaking a woman shall
not be permitted to work during the six weeks following her confinement, shall have the right to leave her
work if she produces a medical certificate stating that
her confinement will probably take place within six
weeks and shall, while she is absent from her work in
accordance with these provisions, be paid benefits
sufficient for the full and healthy maintenance of herself
and her child. Certain provisions of a subsidiary kind
were also included in the Convention with a view to
the further protection of women. It is laid down that
no mistake of a medical officer in estimating the date
of confinement shall preclude a woman from receiving
these benefits from the date of the medical certificate
up to the date on which the confinement actually takes
place. Further, if the woman is actually nursing her
child, she shall be allowed half an hour twice a day
during her working hours for this purpose. In the

third place, it shall not be lawful for an employer to give notice of dismissal to a woman absent from work in accordance with the above provisions or medically certified to be absent on account of causes arising out of her confinement.

Two or three points in connection with this Convention deserve special attention. One is the sources from which maternity benefit should be paid and the fixation of uniform methods for the payment of benefits. Some discussion took place on this point, but eventually the Conference decided that it was impossible to lay down hard and fast rules. It was therefore determined to allow the method to be either direct payment by the State or a system of public insurance, and to prescribe no rule as to amount other than that the Government should order such a rate of benefit to be paid as to provide adequate maintenance for mother and child.

Considerable discussion took place with regard to the length of the period during which a woman should be allowed to remain away from work prior to her confinement. The employers contended that four weeks was not only sufficient, but that medical evidence showed that it would be more favourable to the mother and her child if the period were fixed at four weeks than at six. The employers' contention was, however, defeated by one of those illogical but effective arguments which are often conclusive in any assembly. Miss Mary MacArthur, of Great Britain, suggested that if the employers' contention were justified, their wives equally should profit by the expert medical advice which they quoted and should take employment in factories.

The last point to which attention may be directed is the fact that alone of all the Conventions and Recommendations adopted by the Conference, this Convention applied to commerce as well as to industry. It was clear to the Conference that there was a strong case for such an extension. The number of women employed in commerce greatly exceeds the number employed in industry, and there can hardly be any more unfavourable occupation for a woman approaching her confinement than one which demands many hours of continual standing or walking. The decision, however, to extend the Convention to commerce was taken somewhat hastily by the Conference, without due consideration having been given to the question by the Commission. Whatever opinion be taken as to the merits of the decision, it is clear that it was a misfortune that so important an issue was settled without adequate study or discussion. The years that have passed since the Conference have shown that it was in fact a tactical error to extend the Convention to commerce. Its ratification has been adversely affected in many countries by the disinclination of the countries concerned to include in their legislation provisions with regard to commerce.

*The Employment of Children.*—Two Draft Conventions were also adopted with regard to the employment of children and young persons. The first and most important of these prohibits the employment of children in industry under the age of fourteen. It further provides that in order to facilitate the enforcement of the provisions of the Convention, every employer in an industrial undertaking is required to keep a register of all persons under the age of sixteen years employed by him and of the dates of their births. Many of the members of the Conference would have liked to fix the age higher than fourteen, but the Conference was impressed by the fact that the fixation of the minimum age for the admission of children to employment depends to a very considerable extent on the educational facilities and regulations in the various countries. If the educational regulations of a country provide that education shall be continued only until the age of twelve, then if employment is prohibited before the age of fourteen it is clear that the children will be left for two or three years entirely without regular occupation or supervision. If, as certain members of the Conference would have wished, the minimum age for admission into industry had been fixed at sixteen, it is certain that in a very large number of countries in which the sense of public responsibility for education is not yet sufficiently developed, this intervening period in the child's life would have occurred with results which could hardly be less than disastrous. Fourteen was therefore unanimously adopted as a compromise.

A special provision was inserted in the case of Japan providing that as the school leaving age varies between twelve and fourteen in that country, children who had completed their education might be employed when they reached the age of twelve. In the case of India, it was provided that children under twelve should not be employed in factories using power and employing more than ten persons, in mines, on railways and in docks. This provision was inserted by the Conference in the Convention contrary to the view of the Indian Government delegates, who suggested that any definite decision on the matter should be postponed for a year in order to allow the Indian Government to submit proposals in the light of the scheme for general education which was then under consideration. The Conference, however, felt that immediate steps should be taken to limit the employment of children in factories working under Western conditions.

The other Draft Convention dealt with the employment of young persons in industry during the night. It provides that young persons under eighteen years of age shall not be employed during the night in any public or private industrial undertaking, with the exception that in the case of certain continuous processes young persons of sixteen may be employed. This Convention carries a stage further the principle formulated by the Berne Conference of 1913, according to which night work of young persons under the age of sixteen should be prohibited. In the case of Japan, the limit of age was fixed at fifteen for three years and sixteen thereafter, and in that of India, at eighteen for girls and fourteen for boys.

*Employment in Unhealthy Processes.*—The last of the groups of subjects dealt with by the Conference was that of employment in unhealthy processes. A Commission on Unhealthy Processes, containing a number of well-known medical experts, presented a report with various Recommendations, all of which were adopted by the Conference. The Commission was hampered in its work by the large, and to a great extent unexplored, field comprised in the term " unhealthy processes." The Commission itself had no time to examine in detail the large number of complicated problems involved and it therefore confined itself to clearing the ground for dealing with three of the most dangerous of industrial diseases, namely, carbonic oxide poisoning, lead poisoning and anthrax.

The first of these Recommendations urges members of the Organisation, in view of the danger involved to the function of maternity and to the physical development of children, women and young persons under the age of eighteen years, to exclude them from employment in a number of specified processes in which there is a danger of lead poisoning. The Recommendation further suggests certain precautions where women and young persons are employed in processes involving the use of lead compounds and the compulsory substitution of non-toxic substances for the latter wherever practicable.

In regard to anthrax, the Conference adopted a Recommendation proposing that arrangements should be made for the disinfection of wool infected with anthrax spores either in the country exporting such wool, or, if this is not practicable, at the port of entry, in the country importing such wool.

On the question of carbonic oxide poisoning, no Recommendation was adopted, but a Resolution was approved laying down certain general principles and recommending a further study of them to the International Labour Office with a view to the preparation of a Draft Convention for a further Conference.

Finally, a Recommendation was adopted urging that each member of the International Labour Organisation which had not already done so, should establish as soon as possible not only a system of efficient factory, inspection, but also, in addition thereto, a Government Service especially charged with the duty of safeguarding the health of the workers, which would keep in touch with the International Labour Office.

Another Recommendation was passed urging adherence to the Berne Conference of 1906, prohibiting the use of white phosphorus in the manufacture of matches.

*Conclusions*.—Thus, after less than a month's work, in spite of the great difficulties with which it was faced, the Conference produced twelve detailed constructive international agreements which were adopted not only as the basis, but as the text, of future international action. This was undoubtedly a remarkable result, and it justifies the conclusion that the first Conference was a striking success. It laid the foundation of a system of international labour legislation immeasurably in advance of anything that had been considered possible, even by the most optimistic, before the War.

To some the Conventions may seem unduly moderate in their provisions, but it has to be remembered that the limit of progress in reforms of universal extent is determined in some degree not by the most advanced country, but by the most backward. It was the great work of the Conference to make provision for the gradual, or, in some cases, the rapid raising of the more backward countries to something approaching the level reached in the more advanced countries as a result of years of negotiation and social effort. And if the rate of advance is to some extent conditioned by the most backward countries, it was a great merit of the Conference that it always kept before its eyes, as an ideal, the attainments of the most advanced countries. And one important Convention actually registered an advance on the legislation on the subject then in force even in the most advanced country. In no single country did existing practice cover the entirety of the provisions embodied in the Maternity Convention. On the individual provisions taken separately certain countries have made as generous or even more generous regulations, but the Convention as a whole, by accepting on each point the maximum that seemed genuinely practicable, laid down a standard for dealing with the whole problem more lofty and comprehensive than any national system that then existed.

In three important respects the Washington Conference established a tradition that has been followed by every succeeding Conference. In the first place it demonstrated clearly the possibility of securing agreed results, with unanimity, through compromise. It was clearly evident in the Conference that the diversity of interests and groups was such that without a will to agree, no result could be obtained. The Conference was crossed and re-crossed by important lines of division of interest. These lines of division did not only distinguish workers from employers and both from Governments ; they separated country from country, they divided Europe from America and both from the Orient. But agreement was reached, and in most cases unanimous agreement, because of the readiness of each interest and group to concede a little here in return for a little there, to barter an exception on one point for a stricter regulation on another. It was this interplay of forces, this process of mutual adjustment, which, guided by the spirit of the will to agree, made possible the success of Washington.

Another striking feature of the decisions of the Washington Conference was their precision and detail. Too often assemblies, international as well as national, in which opposing points of view are strongly felt and strongly expressed, are content to reach agreement in some general formula, and to embody it in a vague resolution. But the Draft Conventions and Recommendations of Washington are far from being pious generalities. They are carefully drafted, explicit and detailed. They are solid and workmanlike. They are not loose abstractions, but closely articulated, concrete enactments. Indeed, the only criticism which four years' experience of attempting to apply them in national legislation has produced is that in certain respects the provisions are framed in perhaps too rigid and too inelastic a manner. However that may be, the texts of the Washington decisions proved that the Conference was not an assembly of amiable cranks, but a genuine legislative body composed of practical men of the widest experience in labour and industrial problems.

The last feature of the Conference to which attention may be directed was its wisdom in restricting itself within the limits of its competence. It definitely, though by a narrow majority, declined to concern itself with the question of the distribution of raw materials. It equally definitely declined to venture upon the troubled seas of international emigration or to legislate in detail on the complexities of the prevention of industrial diseases. It declined again to deal with the question of the application of the principle of the eight-hour day to seamen, wisely leaving that to a subsequent Conference of experts. *Ne sutor supra crepidam* is a good motto for any assembly, and the Washington Conference may fairly be said to have observed it. In one case only did it depart from this rule. When it extended the provisions of the Maternity Convention to commerce it was undoubtedly carried away by a wave of sentiment. But this exception only serves to illustrate the strictness with which in general the cobbler stuck to his last.

# CHAPTER V

## THE GENOA CONFERENCE

THE Second Session of the International Labour Conference was held at Genoa from June 15, 1920, to July 10, 1920. This Conference, which was concerned exclusively with the regulation of the conditions of labour at sea, was the direct sequel, not only in time but also in subject, of the Washington Conference. The Washington Conference, in adopting a Draft Convention limiting the hours of work in industrial undertakings to eight in the day and forty-eight in the week, included the transport of passengers by sea or inland waterways amongst the undertakings deemed to be covered by the term " industrial undertaking," but it inserted in the text of the Draft Convention a paragraph to the effect that " the provisions relative to transport by sea and on inland waterways shall be determined by a special Conference dealing with employment at sea and on inland waterways."

Accordingly, the Governing Body of the International Labour Organisation, during its meeting held in Paris on January 26–28, 1920, decided that the Second Session of the Conference should be a special Seamen's Conference and should therefore deal with these problems of employment at sea and on inland waterways. The detailed agenda drawn up by the Governing Body at this meeting was as follows :—

1. Application to seamen of the Convention drafted at Washington last November, limiting the hours of work in all industrial undertakings, including transport by sea and, under conditions

to be determined, transport by inland waterways, to eight hours in the day and forty-eight in the week.

Consequential effects as regards manning and the regulations relating to accommodation and health on board ship.

2. Supervision of articles of agreement. Provision of facilities for finding employment for seamen. Application to seamen of the Convention and Recommendations adopted at Washington in November last in regard to unemployment and unemployment insurance.

3. Application to seamen of the Convention adopted at Washington prohibiting the employment of children under fourteen years of age.

4. Consideration of the possibility of drawing up an International Seamen's Code.

This Conference therefore differs from the Washington Conference in that its agenda was not, like that of the first Conference, determined by the Peace Treaty itself. But its authority did not merely rest on the apostolic succession of the decisions of the Washington Conference and the Governing Body. Its being, like that of Washington, was derived directly from the Peace Conference. For the Commission on International Labour Legislation set up by the Peace Conference decided, on the proposal of the French Delegation, that " the very special questions concerning the minimum conditions to be accorded to seamen might be dealt with at a special meeting of the International Labour Conference devoted exclusively to the affairs of seamen."

The general atmosphere of the Conference did not differ fundamentally from that of Washington. In some respects it appeared, indeed, at first sight more favourable. The special initial difficulties with which, as we have seen, the Washington Conference found itself faced, did not present themselves at Genoa. Further, the Genoa Conference was not, like Washington, a step in the dark into a sphere of unknown dangers. The first Conference had been held, and had been unanimously regarded as a complete success. A valuable tradition of success had thus been established. The immediate problems with which the Conference would have to grapple were less extensive, and even in many respects less complicated, than those of Washington.

And yet, as the Conference proceeded, to the attentive observer it became evident that there was a difference. What exactly this difference was, it would have been difficult to explain. Could it be that the brightness of the ideals which had inspired the proceedings at Washington had slightly paled? Could it be that the ardour for social reform which had led to the birth of the Organisation had now, conscious of the paternity of what might prove an *enfant terrible,* somewhat cooled? In any case, it soon became clear at Genoa that there was a tendency to a sharp opposition of the interests of workers and employers, and a tendency to an emphasis on nationality, both of which were foreign to the spirit of ardent internationalism and social harmony that had reigned at Washington. To what extent these manifestations were due to a weakening of the spiritual ideals of social regeneration which inspired Part XIII of the Peace Treaty, and to what extent to the physical exhaustion of long sessions in the July heat of Genoa, the cautious student of history will hesitate to pronounce.

The Agenda of the Conference was communicated to the States Members of the Organisation on February 3, 1920, and replies to the questionnaires sent out by the Office did not begin to come in till May. Although many were not received till the last moment, the Office was able to present to the Conference four reports on the items on the Agenda, namely: (1) Hours of work at Sea ; (2) Unemployment of Seamen ; (3) Employment of Boys on Board Ship, and (4) An International Maritime Code. While the reports contained most of the information available on the subjects for discussion, it was found that on certain aspects of these questions national legislation was meagre and therefore little assistance could be obtained with a view to the drafting of international conventions.

The Conference was attended by delegates of all the principal maritime countries, with the exception of the United States. In all, 27 States were represented by 87 delegates, of whom 47 represented Governments, 20 shipowners' and 20 seamen's organisations. The fall in the number of countries represented is explained by the specialist character of the Conference, in which non-maritime States naturally took no interest.

As President of the Conference Baron Mayor des Planches was appointed. The choice was a happy one. Baron Mayor des Planches was the Italian Government delegate, and it was therefore appropriate that he should be called on to preside at a session of the Conference held in Italy.

The three Vice-Presidents were M. Arthur Fontaine, French Government delegate, M. Nijgh, Dutch ship-owners' delegate, and Mr. Havelock Wilson, British seamen's delegate. The Secretariat of the Conference was of course drawn from the Staff of the International Labour Office, with the Director at its head as Secretary-General, and the Deputy Director as Deputy Secretary-General.

The system of Commissions and Committees which had proved so successful at Washington was again adopted. Apart from the standing committees of the Conference, the Commission of Selection, the Commission on Credentials and the Drafting Committee, the Conference appointed Commissions to deal with the various questions on the Agenda. These were the Commission on Hours of Labour, the Commission on Unemployment, the Commission on the Minimum Age for the Employment of Children at Sea, the Commission on the International Seamen's Code and the Commission on Inland Navigation. Each of these Commissions proposed Draft Conventions or Recommendations for the adoption of the Conference.

*The Protection of Children.*—An important Draft Convention was adopted fixing the minimum age for the admission of children to employment at sea. This provides that children under the age of fourteen years shall not be employed or work on vessels other than vessels upon which only members of the same family are employed, but that these provisions shall not apply to work done by children on school ships or training ships provided that such work is approved and super-

vised by public authority. For the purpose of the
Convention, it was provided that the term " vessel "
should include all ships and boats of any nature what-
soever engaged in maritime navigation, whether publicly
or privately owned, but should exclude ships of war.
In order to facilitate the enforcement of the provisions
of the Convention, every shipmaster is required by the
terms of the Convention to keep a register of all
persons under the age of sixteen years employed on
board his vessel, or a list of them in the articles of
agreement and of the dates of their birth.

In the course of the discussion on this Convention,
it was pointed out that there were two main reasons for
fixing a minimum age below which children should not
be employed at sea. The first of these related to the
physical development of children. It was considered to
be obviously wrong to expose children below the age
of fourteen years to the hard work and the risk of
diseases such as consumption and bronchitis, to which
sailors are particularly exposed. The Conference was
also moved by the desire to secure that children should
have opportunities to complete their primary education
before going to sea. In this connection, it was pointed
out that in former times, in the days of sailing vessels,
the master of the ship took an interest in the children
and gave them elementary education and perhaps lessons
in navigation. In the days of steam, however, it was
impossible to do this. It was considered essential,
therefore, that children should have up to the age of
fourteen to complete their elementary education before
proceeding to sea.

Efforts were made on the part of the shipowners
in Greece and in India to secure special conditions in
connection with the employment of children in Greece
and in India on the lines of those accorded by the
Washington Conference. It was pointed out by the
Greek shipowners that at the age of twelve in Greece
children were concluding a normal school education, and
in many of the Greek islands, where the great majority
of the people lived by the sea, if children were not

allowed to go to sea before the age of fourteen it would mean that for two years they would live in idleness. It was maintained that these two years of idleness would be more detrimental to the children than life on board ship, where they would generally be under the supervision of their fathers or friends. The Greek Government delegate, however, declined to agree with the employers' delegate.

A request for special treatment somewhat similar to that of the Greek employers' delegate was made by the Indian Government delegate. He pointed out that the Lascar boys who work on Indian ships are not boys casually picked up in the ports, but are those who are brought to sea by their fathers and relatives to serve with a batch of Lascars who come from their own villages. These men are hereditary seamen. Their sons are destined for the sea, and it is regarded as a privilege that they should be allowed, under the guidance of their own people, to learn their own trade by following the sea. In a tropical climate a boy reaches maturity much earlier than in Europe, and it was maintained by the Indian Government delegate that this distinction between India and other countries was on that account justified. This contention was, however, opposed, notably by the Portuguese seafarers' delegate, who pointed out that even though in India a child of twelve years was physically equal to a child of fourteen years in Europe, it was impossible that he could be equal from the moral and intellectual standpoint.

The sense of the Conference was against providing for any special conditions for India, and, as has already been indicated, the Draft Convention as finally adopted excepts no particular country from the general provisions of the Convention.

In the course of the debate on the Draft Convention, it became clear that there were other subjects connected with the legal protection of children employed at sea on which, while the Conference considered that legislation might be desirable, it was not yet prepared to commit itself definitely. On two of these questions it was proposed that a decision should be taken at the next Conference. These were the questions of the medical inspection of children employed at sea and the employment of young persons as trimmers and stokers. It was therefore decided that the Agenda of the next Conference should contain the two following questions:

1. The prohibition of the employment of any person under the age of eighteen years as a trimmer or stoker; and
2. The question of the compulsory medical examination to which all children employed on board should be submitted.

It was also proposed that the Agenda of the next Session of the Conference should consider the question of the prohibition of the employment of persons aged less than seventeen years on night watches, between 8 p.m. and 6 a.m. The Conference, however, decided not to adopt this proposal. It was considerably influenced by the speech of the technical adviser to the German shipowners' delegate, Dr. Ehlers, who pointed out that in the interests of the education in seamanship of a young man of fifteen or sixteen, it was very desirable that he should have an opportunity of going on night watch; and further, that it would be extremely difficult, owing to the way in which night watches are regulated on board ship, to avoid employing young seamen on the night watch. In the interests of the education of young seamen, the Conference passed the following resolution :—

The Conference desires that provision shall be made in all quarters as far as possible, and in any case in those of the principal maritime towns, for the establishment of technical and complementary schools for seamen.

*Unemployment and establishing facilities for finding employment for seamen.*—The Unemployment Commission produced two Draft Conventions, one Recommendation and one Resolution, all of which were adopted either as proposed by the Commission, or with very slight modifications. The most important of these decisions dealt with facilities for finding employment for seamen. This Convention provides that the business of finding employment for seamen shall not be carried on by any person, company or other agency as a commercial enterprise for pecuniary gain, nor shall any fees be charged directly or indirectly by any person, company or other agency for finding employment for seamen on any ship. The law of each country shall provide punishment for any violation of these provisions. The Convention also makes a positive provision with a view to establishing on an equitable basis the facilities required by seamen in order to assist them to find employment. It is provided in the Draft Convention that each Member State of the Organisation ratifying the Convention agrees that there shall be organised and maintained an efficient and adequate system of public employment offices for finding employment for seamen without charge. Such system may be organised and maintained either (1) by representative associations of shipowners and seamen jointly under the control of a central authority, or (2) in the absence of such joint action, by the State itself. It is also provided that the work of all such employment offices shall be administered by persons having practical maritime experience, and that where such employment offices of different types exist, steps shall be taken to co-ordinate them on a national basis. It is further provided, in order that equitable arrangements may be ensured, that committees consisting of an equal number of representatives of shipowners and seamen shall be constituted to advise on matters concerning the carrying on of these offices, and further, that in connection with the employment of seamen, freedom of choice of ship shall be assured to the seamen, and freedom of choice of crew to the shipowners.

An interesting provision of the Draft Convention is that each of the Members ratifying the Convention engages to take steps to see that the facilities for employment of seamen provided for in the Convention shall, if necessary by means of public offices, be available for the seamen of all countries which ratify the Convention and where the industrial conditions are generally the same.

In the course of the debate on the Draft Convention, strong expression was given to the conviction of the Conference that this Convention, by prohibiting the multifarious and noxious activities of the crimp, was doing a great deal for the seamen. It was pointed out by many of the speakers that for many years sailors have been, and still are, largely at the mercy of the crimp when seeking a berth on a ship. The crimp usually runs sailors' rooming and boarding houses and undertakes to furnish shipmasters with crews. The crimping system is responsible for terrible abuses and inhuman practices in securing crews. It has been difficult, even in those countries in which shipowners and seamen are united in desiring the suppression of the crimp, to secure this result, as he is generally a person who plies his calling in many forms and conceals his varied activities with many disguises. Every hope was expressed by the Conference that the provisions of this Convention would definitely succeed in stamping out this pest who battens on the seafarer.

A Draft Convention was also adopted providing that in every case of loss or foundering of any vessel, the owner or person with whom the seaman has contracted for service on board the vessel shall pay each seaman employed thereon an indemnity against unemployment resulting from such loss or foundering. The indemnity shall be paid for the days during which the seaman remains in fact unemployed at the same rate as the wages payable under the contract, but the total indemnity payable under this Convention to one seaman may be limited to two months' wages. Seamen shall have the same remedies for recovering such indemnities as they have for recovering arrears of wages earned during service.

With a view to securing the application to seamen of Part III of the Recommendation concerning unemployment adopted at the Washington Conference, a Recommendation was adopted, which urges that each member of the International Labour Organisation should establish for seamen an effective system of insurance against unemployment arising out of shipwreck or any other cause, either by means of Government insurance or by means of Government subventions to industrial organisations whose rules provide for the payment of benefits to their unemployed members.

The last result of the work of the Unemployment Commission was a resolution which was adopted by the Conference providing that the Joint Maritime Committee established by the Conference should study the question of providing insurance against unemployment for seamen. For this purpose, the Joint Committee should be assisted by the Special Commission on Unemployment set up by the International Labour Office in accordance with the decisions of the Washington Conference.

*Hours of Labour.*—The most important question on the Agenda was undoubtedly that of the application to seamen of the Draft Convention adopted at Washington, limiting the hours of work in all industrial undertakings, including transport by sea, and, under conditions to be determined, transport by inland waterways, to eight hours in the day and forty-eight in the week. On this question, after a discussion lasting some four weeks, it was finally found impossible to reach any agreement. The final vote provided the most dramatic incident in the history of the Organisation. Forty-eight delegates voted for and twenty-five against a Draft Convention, which thus failed to be carried by the necessary two-thirds majority by only two-thirds of a vote.

But although the result of the debates on this most important matter was negative, the discussions themselves were both interesting and instructive to the student of the international regulation of conditions of labour.

In order to understand clearly the difficulties with which the Conference had to contend, it is necessary to bear in mind in the first place the precise relation of the Genoa Conference on this matter to that of Washington.

The Commission which prepared the Draft Convention on Hours of Labour that was adopted by the Washington Conference recommended that the principles of the eight-hour day and the forty-eight-hour week should be accepted as the general basis for revision of the hours of work for seamen, just as they were accepted by the Peace Conference as the basis for revision of the hours of work for industrial workers on shore. But just as the Peace Conference made no attempt to work out the practical application of these principles to shore industries, but referred the task to the Washington Conference, so the Washington Conference in its turn made no attempt to apply them to the maritime services of the world, but referred the whole question to a special conference which would consist mainly of persons familiar with maritime conditions and therefore competent to deal with the various technical difficulties attending a reduction of the hours of work at sea. It is clear, therefore, that the Washington Convention does not definitely establish an eight-hour day and a forty-eight-hour week for seamen. It only indicates these daily and weekly periods as being the limits which should be kept in view as desirable so far as the special circumstances of maritime employment permit. That this was the intention of the Convention may be further illustrated by observing the method by which it applies the same principle to shore industry. The Convention does not prescribe a rigid eight-hour day and forty-eight-hour week for all industries. On the contrary, it permits a normal week of fifty-six hours in processes carried on continuously by a succession of shifts, and it also permits a nine-hour day to be worked within certain limits in cases where the Saturday half-holiday is observed. This and other provisions of the Convention exhibit the conviction of the Washington Conference that in applying the principles of the eight-hour day and forty-eight-hour week to meet the actual conditions of industry, considerable modifications and important exceptions are inevitable. In applying them to sea service, it was recognised that similar modifications and exceptions would probably be necessary. The Washington Conference, which did not include technical experts on matters relating to conditions of work at sea, therefore left the special Seamen's Conference free to introduce such modifications and exceptions as it might think necessary.

If the precise nature of the relationship which has just been indicated had been clearly realised by all present at Genoa, much of the discussion which took place on the Commission and in the Conference would have been avoided. As it was, the Commission on Hours of Labour and the Conference itself were torn between the opposing views on the one hand of the workers and employers, and on the other hand of groups of Governments led respectively by the French and British. The seamen's view in general was that the provisions of the Washington Convention on Hours of Labour should apply practically without alteration to the conditions of work of seamen. The shipowners, on the other hand, contended that the Genoa Conference should be left completely free to adopt any decision on the matter that it chose to approve, in complete independence of the decisions of Washington.

The Government delegates, as so frequently happens at the Conference, attempted to reach a compromise which would be acceptable to both the extreme parties. Unfortunately, however, the Governments themselves were not in agreement. A sharp cleavage of opinion early manifested itself between the point of view of the British Government, supported in general by the Northern countries, Japan and Spain, and that of the French Government, supported by most of the other countries. The French system provided for a forty-eight-hour week with unlimited overtime, compensated by additional wages or by off-time if in port. On the other hand, the British Government proposed a fifty-six-hour week at sea and a forty-eight-hour week in port, with strict limitation of overtime.

The result of the voting on the first and second articles of the Convention finally submitted by the Commission to the Conference, which embodied the French system, was such as to indicate that it was unlikely that the Convention would secure the necessary two-

thirds majority.  A proposal was therefore made to refer
the whole Convention back to the Commission with a
view to seeing if some agreement could be reached in
Commission.  The Conference, however, was anxious
to finish its work and appeared, further, to be somewhat
suspicious of the negotiations which might take place
in Commission.  It preferred to keep the decision openly
in its own hands and therefore proceeded directly to
vote on the Convention as a whole after the usual vote
by articles had taken place.  The result, as has already
been indicated, was as anticipated, namely, the Convention failed of final acceptance by a fraction of a vote.

The disappointment of those who were most interested in the future of the Organisation at this result
was at the time intense.  But from a distance of three
years it is now possible to see that this apparently
negative result was in reality the best for the prestige
of the Organisation as a whole.  For if the Convention
had been adopted, it is certain that several of the most
important maritime countries which voted in the
minority, including Great Britain, Japan, Norway and
Spain, would not have ratified the Convention.  This
result would have been more inimical to the principle
of agreement upon labour legislation through international conferences than the failure of the Conference
to reach a decision upon one item, however important,
on its Agenda.

*International Seamen's Code.*—Perhaps the most
interesting question on the Agenda from the standpoint, not of its immediate practical importance, but its
genuine international significance, was that of the
consideration of the possibility of drawing up an
international seamen's code.

The information collected by the Office before the
Conference indicated that a considerable amount of
national legislation was in force in the principal maritime countries relating to the matters on which the
conclusion of international agreements seemed to be
most practicable, as, for instance, articles of agreement,
manning and accommodation.  The provisions concern-

ing articles of agreement in particular appeared to be specially susceptible of international codification owing to their formal nature.

A study of the national legislation showed that measures with regard to articles of agreement are formal, in the sense that they provide that definite legal agreements shall be made between master and seamen, and they lay down the conditions under which binding agreements shall be made, but they do not deal with the actual content of the terms of the agreement. It is stipulated for example in most laws on this subject, that the amount of the wages which each seaman is to receive shall be entered in the agreement ; but the provisions with regard to articles of agreement have nothing to do with the determination of the actual wage to be paid. In this sense, then, the question of articles of agreement is a formal one.

The general view of the States which expressed their opinions before the Conference on the possibility of an international code for seamen was that there were no insuperable difficulties in the way of an international code for seamen. They considered, however, that the time was not yet ripe, owing to the variety and the complexity of the problems involved, for the detailed discussion of the project.

At the Conference this general standpoint was confirmed. The Commission on the International Seamen's Code in its report pointed out that in most countries the systematic codification of seamen's law had not yet been undertaken, with the result that there was frequently confusion in the minds of seamen, if not also in the minds of shipowners, as to the precise nature of their rights and obligations. The British Merchant Shipping Act of 1894, and the German Seamen's Law of 1902 could, indeed, in a sense be called national seamen's codes, but even these compilations of the laws relating to seamen were not complete, and progress had still to be made even in these countries towards a more complete systematisation of seamen's law.

The Commission was convinced that it would greatly

facilitate the establishment of an international seamen's code if each of the maritime countries of the world would advance so far as possible the codification of its own law relating to seamen.  The clear and systematic statement of the law of each country in a single compilation would make it much easier for it to be understood in other countries.  The uniformity that already exists would be more easily extended if such national codification were effected.

The Commission therefore decided to urge that the Conference should adopt a Recommendation in this sense.  This Recommendation was duly adopted by the Conference.  It runs as follows :—

In order that, as a result of the clear and systematic codification of the national law in each country, the seamen of the world, whether engaged on ships of their own or foreign countries, may have a better comprehension of their rights and obligations, and in order that the task of establishing an International Seamen's Code may be advanced and facilitated, the International Labour Conference recommends that each Member of the International Labour Organisation undertake the embodiment in a seamen's code of all its laws and regulations relating to seamen in their activities as such.

The Commission in its Report further pointed out that certain advances in the direction of an international code for seamen had already been made, such as the Consolato del Mare in the Middle Ages for the Mediterranean countries, and the Inter-Scandinavian Maritime Law of 1893.  The Commission was therefore of opinion that there was nothing inherently impossible in the drafting of an international code, provided that it should be framed in elastic terms and that provision for periodical consideration and revision should be made.

The Commission pointed out two main possible advantages to be expected from the establishment of an international seamen's code.  In the first place, seamen, unlike workers in many other fields, often had to do their work in several countries, in each of which it might be necessary for them to know something of the law as to their relations with their employers and their fellows. Even when not in other countries, much of the seamen's work must be done on the world's highway, far removed from the usual reach of public authorities. Moreover, on the ships of most countries, the seamen are frequently of many nationalities. It is not unusual that the seamen on a ship neither speak the language of the ship's country, nor understand its laws. Seamen form what is indeed an international community, and as such they have many relations in which it would be much to their advantage to have a uniform law applied to them to avoid conflict or confusion in the vessel in which they ship. This uniform law could be secured only through common international action.

Another advantage, the Commission pointed out, was quite as obvious and quite as important. In view of the keenness of commercial competition between the merchant fleets of various countries, there are certain fields in which various States find it difficult to adopt any new legislation because of its possible reaction to the advantage of the merchant fleet of a competing country. If, for instance, one State attempts by legislation to secure the improvement of the seamen's living accommodation, it may find itself at a disadvantage vis-à-vis another State which fails or refuses to make a similar change in its laws. Commerce tends to apportion itself among States in accordance with the advantages and disadvantages in existing legislation, and the balance which is thus struck at any one time is frequently a very delicate and precarious one which any change in legislation may upset. Progress in national law will therefore depend to a large extent upon the possibility of common international action in a particular legislative field, and without such international action, the progress which is possible may be precluded altogether.

The Commission further pointed out that the work of actually codifying the legislation would be work of many years, and it therefore proposed to the Conference five specially promising fields for further investigation and possible codification. These were :—

1. Articles of agreement.
2. Accommodation for seamen aboard vessels.
3. Discipline.
4. Settlement of disputes between individual seamen and their employers.
5. Social and industrial insurance for seamen and possible arrangements for international reciprocity in this field.

Investigation of what has been done in these fields has since been continued by the Joint Maritime Commission of the International Labour Office.

*The Limitation of Hours of Work in the Fishing Industry.*—One of the questions of minor importance discussed by the Conference was the problem how far workers employed in the fishing industry should be included in the decisions of the Conference. Several speakers from various countries pointed out that the conditions of work in the fishing industry were extremely technical and varied much, not only from country to country, but from district to district in the same country, and there appeared to be general agreement that in view of the fact that no fishermen's representatives were present at the Conference, it would be unwise for the Conference to enter into any detailed discussion of the regulation of work in the fishing industry. Mr. Henson, of Great Britain, pointed out that for several years in England attempts had been made to reach not an international agreement but a national agreement so far as hours of labour and conditions are concerned. In view of the great technical difficulties involved, it had not been possible even to reach a national agreement in the case of one country. A French seamen's technical adviser, M. Réaud, pointed out that in France it had been impossible to reach a national agreement, and it had been necessary to depend on purely local agreements as regards coast fishing. The special difficulties in the way of the regulation of working conditions in the fishing industry were also pointed out by Mr. Hipwood, one of the Government representatives of Great Britain. He pointed out that coast fishing and in-shore fishing differs very much in different countries. Further, this type of fishing differs entirely from deep-sea fishing undertaken by the trawler and the drifter. Further, a number of the fishing trades are seasonal in character and in many cases boats are owned by a family, or partly owned by a family. The men are themselves both employers and employees. His view, therefore, was that it would be impossible for the Conference to deal with such a trade, especially in the absence of a representative of the trade. Eventually, after some further discussion, it was agreed that the Conference should adopt a general recommendation. This Recommendation is as follows :—

In view of the declaration in the Treaties of Peace that all industrial communities should endeavour to adopt, so far as their special circumstances will permit, " an eight-hours' day or a forty-eight-hours' week as the standard to be aimed at where it has not already been attained," the International Labour Conference recommends that each Member of the International Labour Organisation enact legislation limiting in this direction the hours of work of all workers employed in the fishing industry, with such special provisions as may be necessary to meet the conditions peculiar to the fishing industry in each country : and that in framing such legislation each Government consult with the organisations of employers and the organisations of workers concerned.

*Inland Navigation.*—Another minor question affecting the scope of the Conference was the extent to which it should deal with questions relating to conditions of work in inland navigation. Monsignor Nolens, the Government delegate of the Netherlands, was in favour of the making of definite regulations for inland water navigation by the Conference, in view of the fact that it was apparently the intention of the Washington Conference that the Genoa Conference should include the question of inland water transport. The general view of the delegates was, however, opposed to this.

It was pointed out that it was extremely difficult to define with precision what was meant by inland water transport. In the first place, inland water transport might be divided into three main classes—canal transport, river transport and transport on large lakes. The conditions in each of these three classes of navigation

vary very much. Further, the same boat, in the course
of its work, passes through various countries. Boats
may pass by canal between France, Germany, Belgium
and Holland. Again, navigation on rivers and
lakes in some cases is quite akin to ordinary
sea navigation. In the case of the St. Lawrence,
for example, it was pointed out that ships cover
a distance of 2,000 miles from New Brunswick to
Lake Superior, all of which was inland water transport. The conditions of such long voyages are more
akin to those of ordinary sea transport than in cases
where boats navigate a few miles on a short river.
One of the Canadian delegates pointed out that in view
of the importance of inland water transport in the United
States, it would be a very serious matter to make any
detailed recommendation for the regulation of conditions
of work in inland water transport without the representation of the United States. It was agreed that the
position with regard to inland water transport was
somewhat different from that with regard to fishing,
inasmuch as a certain number of the delegates were
experts with regard to this question. In the end, however, it was decided that it would be best simply to
adopt a recommendation of a general character concerning the limitation of hours of work in inland
navigation. This Recommendation begins by drawing
attention to the declaration in the Treaty of Peace that
all industrial communities should adopt, so far as their
special circumstances should permit, " an eight-hours'
day or a forty-eight-hours' week as a standard to be
aimed at where it has not already been attained." It
goes on to recommend that each Member of the International Labour Organisation should communicate legislation limiting in the direction of the above declaration
in the Treaty of Peace the hours of work of workers
employed in inland navigation, with such special provisions as may be necessary to meet the climatic and
industrial conditions peculiar to inland navigation in
each country, and after consultation with the organisations of employers and the organisations of workers

concerned. The Recommendation includes also the following provisions :—

That those Members of the International Labour Organisation whose territories are riparian to waterways which are used in common by their boats should enter into agreements for limiting, in the direction of the aforesaid declaration, the hours of work of persons employed in inland navigation on such waterways, after consultation with the organisations of employers and the organisations of workers concerned.

That such national legislation and such agreements between riparian countries should follow as far as possible the general lines of the Draft Convention concerning hours of work adopted by the International Labour Conference at Washington, with such exceptions as may be necessary for meeting the climatic or other special conditions of the countries concerned.

That, in the application of this recommendation, each Member of the International Labour Organisation should determine for itself, after consultation with the organisations of employers and the organisations of workers concerned, what is inland navigation as distinguished from maritime navigation, and should communicate its determination to the International Labour Office.

The decisions of the Genoa Session, important as they are, do not entitle it to a high place in the apostolic succession of the Conference. Carved on the lid of an old chest in the Palazzo San Giorgio, in which the Conference met, was to be seen the following motto:

Ubi ordo deficit nullus virtus sufficit.

There was the secret of the comparative failure of the Conference. It possessed " every virtue, every grace "—except system.

# CHAPTER VI

## THE GENEVA CONFERENCES

THE Third Session of the Conference was held at Geneva, the seat of the Office, from October 25 to November 18, 1921. While this Conference will be noted in history primarily for the variety and extent of its Agenda and for the number and scope of its decisions, two particular features were enough to give it a special pedestal in the pantheon of international labour legislation. The first was the remarkable example of a compromise decision, reached after the most violent conflict of opposing interests, in the White Lead Draft Convention. The other was the brilliant debate with regard to the competence of the Organisation in matters relating to agricultural labour.

The 1921 Conference was, like the Genoa Conference, largely a legacy of the Washington Conference. Most of the items on the Agenda appeared there as a consequence of the work of that Conference. A motion at Washington to include agricultural questions on the Agenda of the next Session of the Conference received a large majority. Although subsequently this vote was invalidated because a quorum was not present, it was considered by the Governing Body as a sufficiently strong indication of the desires of the Washington Conference to justify its insertion on the Agenda of the 1921 Session. The prevention of anthrax appeared on the programme in view of the fact that it had been understood by the Washington Conference which adopted a Recommendation on the question that the matter should be taken up by the Third Session. The question of the use of white lead in painting was placed on

the Agenda as a result of the desire expressed by the
Commission on Unhealthy Processes of that Conference
that the matter should be considered by the next
Conference.

Thus the most important items on the Agenda found
a place there in deference to the views, explicit or
implied, of the parent Conference.

The general atmosphere of the Conference was in
some ways even less favourable to success than at
Washington or Genoa.  The general spirit of optimism
which pervaded the world in 1919 had given place to
doubt, and in some cases to worse than doubt.  Had
peace made the world safe for democracy?  Were
employers and workers finding in co-operation the
solution of their conflicts?  The delegate who asked
himself these questions looked out upon a world
suffering from an unemployment crisis of unexampled
intensity, producers and consumers alike tossed about
in a mad whirl of rising and falling prices, of alternate
glut and famine, boom and slump.  In these circumstances it was difficult even for those who had most
closely at heart the future of the Organisation to remain
loyal to its high ideals : what President Wilson had
called " the tide rising in the hearts of men " appeared
to be definitely on the ebb.  It was a moment of reaction, of disillusion and of doubt ; and the historian
of the future may possibly find that the severest test
in the history of the Organisation was imposed in
October 1921.

Apart from the general spirit of hesitancy, of luke-
warmness and of doubt, danger to the Conference was
to be expected from two particular directions.  In the
first place, a vigorous campaign had been inaugurated
against the intervention of the International Labour
Organisation in the affairs of agricultural workers.  The
lead in this campaign was taken by the Swiss Peasants'
Union, an association of peasant farmers, who protested
vigorously against the proposal to regulate the hours
of labour in agriculture.  The Swiss peasants received
support from the French associations of farmers and

peasants, who considered that it was not opportune that this question should be considered. The agitation in France even led to a decision to question the competence of the Organisation to deal with any agricultural questions whatever. Nor were these associations alone in casting a doubt on the competence of the Organisation. It was clear when the Conference opened that the strongest efforts would be made to declare that the Organisation was incompetent in such matters, and thus to torpedo the Conference in its most vulnerable spot.

A further question had aroused great controversy and vigorous opposition, particularly in Great Britain and Germany. This was the question of the prohibition of the use of white lead in painting. Those interested in the manufacture of white lead feared that the very existence of the industry was menaced, and they made no secret of their intention to oppose with all the power at their command any proposal for a radical prohibition of this material.

The prospects of the Conference could hardly have been more sombre. Yet, as is so frequently the case, the effect of opposition was to convert the lukewarm into ardent partisans, to transmute doubt into conviction and to substitute for hesitancy a spirit of confidence and determination.

The delegates to the Conference numbered 118, and they were accompanied by some 230 technical advisers. The delegates came from 39 States, 69 delegates representing the Governments, and the rest the employers and the workers. A peculiarly prominent part was played in the Conference by the technical advisers. These were of many types—Government officials, factory inspectors, scientists, labour leaders and trade union officials. In the Commissions, owing to their wide and profound technical knowledge, they played important and possibly decisive rôles, and even in the Conference, in which they act as deputies to the delegates, their importance was extremely great.

The Conference was particularly fortunate in its

President, Lord Burnham, the British parliamentarian, and proprietor of the *Daily Telegraph,* well versed in parliamentary procedure, and a man of ready and impartial judgment. Lord Burnham, in a conference in which it was particularly difficult to secure system and expedition, contributed greatly to the success of its work.

The Conference wisely began its labours by tackling directly the problems raised by the objections put forward with regard to its own competence in agricultural matters. M. Arthur Fontaine, as chief French Government delegate, formally moved the deletion from the Agenda of the items concerning agriculture. The memorandum of the French Government which M. Fontaine read referred to the doubts which had been expressed regarding the competence of the Organisation in the matter of the regulation of agricultural labour, and although M. Justin Godart, the second French Government delegate, declared formally that his Government had demanded the withdrawal of these items only on the ground of expediency, the discussion which took place was predominantly concerned with the question of competence. The eloquence of the Conference was chiefly directed towards the defence of the thesis of competence. The workers' delegates, as was to be expected, were unanimously against the idea of incompetence. Their spokesman, M. Jouhaux, in a ringing speech, adduced evidence as to the intentions of the framers of Part XIII of the Peace Treaty. On wider grounds his arguments were reinforced in a convincing speech by Sir Daniel Hall, one of the British Government delegates. Sir Daniel Hall drew attention to the fact that there were millions of agricultural workers throughout the world in receipt of wages. "Are we," he said, "to go back to those men and to say that they are out of court in all international considerations, that their case may never be put here, that they have no status whatever, that they are, as it were, internationally speaking, outlawed? Again, are we to tell the women of many countries who complain that by old custom they are involved in

8

bad conditions of labour, that they can never put their case because they happen to be engaged in agriculture, that though there may be measures drawn up for the protection of women against these evils in industrial matters, yet this Parliament, the one Labour Parliament of the world, will refuse to consider women and the women's case if those women are engaged in agriculture? It is altogether contrary to the interests of agriculture anywhere in the world that we should deny them a statement of their case at a meeting of this description."

Finally, after a valuable debate, the competence of the Organisation was affirmed by a resolution which was adopted by 74 votes to 20.

Further sittings were devoted to the discussion of the expediency of retaining certain questions with regard to agricultural labour on the Agenda. In the end, it was decided that Item 2 on the Agenda, " The adaptation to agricultural labour of the Washington decisions concerning the regulation of the hours of work," should be deleted. The Conference was led to take this decision owing to the feeling of a sufficient proportion of its members that the necessity of feeding a famished and suffering world rendered inopportune any proposal which might result in the restriction of agricultural production.

### Agricultural Questions.

As has already been suggested, the Conference was largely concerned with matters of interest to agricultural workers. On these questions no fewer than three Draft Conventions and seven Recommendations were finally adopted by the Conference.

*Unemployment.*—The question of unemployment was envisaged by the Conference from the point of view of the permanent prevention of unemployment rather than the adoption of proposals of an immediately remedial type. A Recommendation was finally adopted by the Conference which urged each Member of the

Organisation to consider measures for the prevention of unemployment amongst agricultural workers suitable to the economic and agricultural conditions of its country, and to examine particularly from this point of view the advisability of encouraging improved technical methods by which unworked or partially worked land might be brought under cultivation, of encouraging land settlement, of affording transport facilities for the movement of unemployed agricultural workers, of developing supplementary forms of employment in cases of seasonal industries and of encouraging co-operative action by the provision of credits.

*Workmen's Compensation.*—A Draft Convention was adopted concerning workmen's compensation in agriculture, according to which Members of the Organisation undertake to extend to all agricultural wage-earners their laws and regulations which provide for the compensation of workers for personal injury by accident arising out of or in the course of their employment.

*Social Insurance in Agriculture.*—A Recommendation was adopted urging each Member of the Organisation to extend its laws and regulations establishing systems of insurance against sickness, invalidity, old age and other similar social risks to agricultural wage-earners on conditions equivalent to those prevailing in the case of workers in industrial and commercial occupations.

*Protection of Women and Children.*—A number of the decisions of the Conference dealt with the particularly important question of the protection of women and children. These comprised in general the adaptation to agricultural labour of various decisions of the Washington Conference. In some cases the decisions of the Washington Conference were directly applied to agricultural labour, in other cases it was found necessary to modify and adapt these provisions in varying degrees.

The protection of women before and after childbirth was the subject of a Draft Convention at Washington. Although influential sections of the Geneva Conference wished to secure a Draft Convention

couched precisely in the same terms as those of
the Washington Convention, which, it will be remembered, applies not only to industry but also to commerce,
it was eventually decided that only a Recommendation
of a more general kind could be adopted to provide
for the application of this principle in agriculture. The
Recommendation finally adopted urges Members of the
Organisation to take measures to ensure to women
wage-earners employed in agricultural undertakings
protection before and after childbirth similar to that
provided by the Draft Convention adopted by the International Labour Conference at Washington for women
employed in industry and commerce, and provides that
such measures should include the right to a period of
absence from work before and after childbirth, and to
a grant of benefit during the said period provided
either out of public funds or by means of a system
of insurance. It will be noted that this Recommendation does not lay down a fixed period during which
absence from work should be permissible or compulsory.

With regard to the night work of women, on which
the Washington Conference had adopted a Draft
Convention, it was found equally impossible at Geneva
to secure sufficient support for the adoption of a
Draft Convention extending to agricultural women
workers the benefits of the Washington Convention.
The Recommendation eventually adopted by the Conference was much more elastic than the Washington
Convention. This was due in large part to consideration of the dependence of agricultural labour upon
weather conditions and the impossibility of work during
the middle of the day in some climates. The Recommendation provides for a period of rest during the
night of not less than nine hours, if possible consecutive,
instead of the eleven consecutive hours decreed by the
Washington Conference.

With reference to the night work of children, the
decision of the Conference again differed from that
of Washington. It will be remembered that the Draft
Convention adopted at Washington applied to young

persons under eighteen years of age, and provided that they should have a night rest of at least eleven consecutive hours. At Geneva a distinction was made, in the Recommendation which was adopted, between workers under fourteen years of age who are to be ensured a period of rest compatible with their physical necessities and consisting of not less than ten consecutive hours, and those between fourteen and eighteen, for whom the period named is nine hours.

On the important question of the age for admission of children to employment in agriculture, a Draft Convention was adopted. The Conference felt that it was important that the decision adopted should take the somewhat stringent form of a Draft Convention, but it was equally convinced that it was necessary to give to its terms more elasticity than that of the Washington Convention. It is provided that children under the age of fourteen years may not be employed in any public or private agricultural undertaking save outside the hours fixed for school attendance, and it is further laid down that if they are employed outside the hours of school attendance, the employment shall not be such as to prejudice their attendance at school. A certain elasticity is provided for purposes of practical vocational instruction by permitting the employment of children on light agricultural work, and in particular on light work connected with the harvest, provided that such employment shall not reduce the total annual period of school attendance to less than eight months. The general sense of the Conference was that the matter of main importance was to prevent any prejudice to the education of children owing to any light tasks that they might be called upon to do on the farm. It was realised by most of the practical agriculturists present that young children might be called upon outside the hours of school attendance to do small tasks on the farm which would not only be of use to them from the point of view of practical instruction, but were also of a character which might be considered in other circumstances as relaxation.

*Living-in Conditions.*—A particularly difficult problem resulted in a Recommendation concerning the living-in conditions of agricultural workers.  This subject falls a little outside the scope of those which had so far been considered by the International Labour Conference.  The justification for legislation on this subject was, of course, the securing of conditions morally and hygienically healthy.  The Commission which considered the matter found that it was more than usually difficult to elaborate detailed provisions with regard to the accommodation to be provided for agricultural workers.  To a European it would appear obvious that the minimum of accommodation is a bed, but it was pointed out by delegates from the Eastern countries that in many countries a simple mat which can be rolled up suffices for sleeping purposes.  The Recommendation finally agreed upon is therefore drawn in wide terms.  Its detailed provisions are worth quoting, in view of the fact that they established principles which were regarded by the Conference as the minimum necessary for ordinary decent comfort.  There is no doubt that difficulty would be met with in the stringent application of legislation adopted with a view to giving effect to these principles owing to the difficulty of securing inspection of living quarters without offending the sense of personal liberty.

That such measures shall apply to all accommodation provided by employers for housing their workers either individually, or in groups, or with their families, whether the accommodation is provided in the houses of such employers or in buildings placed by them at the workers' disposal.

That such measures shall contain the following provisions :—

(*a*) Unless climatic conditions render heating superfluous, the accommodation intended for workers' families, groups of workers, or individual workers, should contain rooms which can be heated.

(*b*) Accommodation intended for groups of workers shall provide a separate bed for each worker, shall afford facilities for ensuring personal cleanliness, and shall provide for the separation of the sexes.  In the case of families, adequate provision shall be made for the children.

(*c*) Stables, cowhouses and open sheds should not be used for sleeping quarters.

*Technical Agricultural Education.*—No doubt existed in the mind of the Conference as to the desirability of the development of vocational agricultural education. On the other hand, differences in the general level of education in many of the chief agricultural countries made it impossible for the Conference to lay down detailed regulations on this subject. It therefore contented itself with the adoption of a Recommendation urging each Member of the Organisation to endeavour to develop vocational agricultural education, and in particular to make such education available to agricultural wage-earners on the same conditions as to other persons engaged in agriculture.

*Rights of Association and Combination of Agricultural Workers.*—Considerable discussion took place with regard to assuring to agricultural workers rights of association and combination. In the end the Conference adopted a Draft Convention providing that each State undertakes to secure to all those engaged in agriculture the same rights of association and combination as to industrial workers, and to repeal any statutory or other provisions restricting such rights in the case of those engaged in agriculture. Efforts were made by the workers' representatives to extend in two or three directions the scope of this Draft Convention. It was proposed in the first place that the granting of the rights of association and combination should be absolute, and should not be limited to such rights as are enjoyed by industrial workers. The workers' representatives wished to add explicitly also the right of meeting. It was felt, however, by a majority that this was primarily a matter for the internal police arrangements of each country, and that on this question each Government should be left free to judge for itself.

Special reference may be made to the fact that it was agreed by the Conference as a matter of interpretation that the words " all those engaged in agriculture " should be taken to include small peasant farmers and owners as well as wage-earners.

### MARITIME QUESTIONS.

Two important Draft Conventions were adopted on maritime questions. Both of these had been referred to the Geneva Conference by the Second Session of the Conference held at Genoa.

The first of these Draft Conventions provides that the employment of young persons under the age of eighteen as trimmers and stokers is forbidden, with certain well-defined exceptions, such as on school ships, on vessels mainly propelled by other means than steam, and in the Indian and Japanese coasting trade.

The second Draft Convention provides for the medical examination of young seamen. It stipulates that the employment of any child or young person under eighteen years of age on any vessel other than vessels upon which only members of the same family are employed shall be conditional on the production of a medical certificate attesting fitness for such work and continued employment at sea shall be subject to a repetition of such medical examination at intervals of not more than one year and the production of a further medical certificate after each such examination attesting fitness for such work.

Neither of these Draft Conventions extends to the fishing industry. It will be remembered that at the Genoa Session of the Conference the regulation of labour on fishing vessels had been shown to be a specially difficult problem. In this the Geneva Conference concurred and therefore resolved that none of the decisions of the Conference regarding maritime affairs should cover the fishing industry.

### OTHER QUESTIONS.

*Weekly Rest.*—Contrary to expectation, one of the most difficult tasks before the Conference proved to be the reaching of an agreement on the terms of the Draft Convention with regard to the provision of a weekly rest. No doubt was felt with regard to the principle, but serious difficulties emerged in connection

with the drafting of details. To a certain extent, the
weekly rest is the complement of the eight-hour day
and the forty-eight-hour week, and the difficulties which
had arisen in the application of the Washington Convention on this subject had a sinister repercussion on
the problem of the weekly rest. The division of opinion
among the delegates was chiefly between the representatives of the Governments and the employers on
the one hand, who desired to draft the Convention
in as general and elastic a form as possible, and the
workers on the other, who desired to secure definite
and closely binding regulations. In the end a Draft
Convention was adopted which provides that the whole
of the staff employed in any industrial undertaking
shall enjoy in every period of seven days a period of
rest comprising at least twenty-four consecutive hours.
The period of rest, wherever possible, is to be granted
simultaneously to the whole of the staff of each undertaking, and to be fixed so as to coincide wherever
possible with the traditions or customs of the country
or district. Each State may authorise total or partial
exceptions, including suspensions or diminutions. The
following provision, however, is added with regard to
such cases :—

   Special regard being had to all proper humanitarian and economic
considerations and after consultation with responsible associations
of employers and workers wherever such exist.

   Each Member is bound to make, as far as possible,
provision for periods of rest to compensate for the
suspensions or diminutions allowed.
   This Draft Convention applies only to industry.
With regard to the weekly rest in commerce, only a
Recommendation was adopted by the Conference which,
while urging the establishment of a twenty-four hours'
rest, left the making of exceptions entirely to the dis-
cretion of Governments without specifying any limitations whatever.
   As an ideal to be attained at some future date,
the Conference adopted a general resolution urging the

extension of the regular period of weekly rest to thirty-six hours.

*Prohibition of the Use of White Lead in Painting.*— Controversy prior to the Conference had, as has been indicated above, been particularly acute in connection with the question of the prohibition of the use of white lead in painting. It was therefore fortunate that the Commission appointed to deal with the question at Geneva was an exceedingly able one, comprising experts in the technique of painting and paint manufacture, factory inspectors and medical specialists on lead poisoning.

On the Commission the controversy mainly raged around the question of prohibition on the one hand and regulation on the other. In order, however, that the most exact possible scientific basis might be discovered before any decision should be reached, the Commission entrusted to a Medical Sub-Commission the preliminary task of examining whether, in the present state of medical science, it was possible correctly to diagnose lead poisoning. The conclusion was a decided affirmative, and the ground was thereby clear for discussion of the reliability of published statistics of lead poisoning. A second Medical Sub-Commission therefore examined the question of the degree of risk run by painters in the pursuit of their occupation, and the manner in which the poison entered their bodies. The conclusions of this Sub-Commission were likewise clear. Lead poisoning, it was agreed, is the principal risk incurred by the working painter, and the lead generally reaches the system of the worker by way of the mouth and nose, i.e. with his food and drink or with the air he breathes, in the form of dust.

The next question for decision was whether in fact efficient substitutes could be obtained for white lead, providing its use were abolished. On this point, evidence was notably conflicting. Men of wide experience pronounced strongly in favour of certain substitutes. Others were equally convinced that nothing had yet been put forward which could replace white lead. The general sense of the Conference, as is indicated by the Convention, would appear to be that zinc white approaches white lead very closely for interior painting, but that for outside work, or work exposed to fumes or moisture, white lead is superior.

Two further points were debated in Commission. The supporters of regulation rather than prohibition suggested that dry rubbing down—admittedly the most dangerous process in connection with lead painting— was no longer necessary in view of recent experiments with wet rubbing down by means of waterproof sand- paper. Doubt was, however, felt, particularly by the workers' delegates, as to the technical efficiency of this method. The other question discussed by the Commission was the effect of prohibition on the lead- mining industry, one-fifth of the product of which, it was stated, went to the manufacture of paints. It was urged that if prohibition were adopted, the result would be the closing down of many mines, a consequence which would have repercussions in unexpected directions.

The Commission finally decided in favour of regula- tion, as opposed to prohibition, but by so narrow a majority that the leaders in the movement for pro- hibition felt justified in renewing the campaign in the Conference itself. To that end they submitted a minority report. In the Conference itself, however, M. Justin Godart submitted an alternative Draft Con- vention based on the principle of prohibition. This was adopted as a basis of discussion, after amendments had been made, in preference to that submitted by the majority of the Commission. The voting, however, was so close—45 to 44—that it was clear that such a Convention could not hope to be adopted by the Con- ference with the necessary two-thirds majority. In the end a further compromise was reached as a result, in the first place, of an informal discussion between the leaders of the various groups.

The Draft Convention as finally adopted prohibits, with certain exceptions, the use of white-lead paints in interior work, but permits its use, under regulation, for outdoor operations. On the other hand the employment, even in exterior work, of all women and of young persons under eighteen years of age is forbidden, except in the case of apprentices, for whom some elasticity is permitted in the interest of their trade education. A further Article of the Convention aims at securing statistics of morbidity and mortality in connection with lead poisoning among working painters. The Convention is to become effective at the earliest in 1927.

This Convention, like most legislation and most collective agreements, is a compromise, but if ratified it will represent a marked advance in industrial sanitary regulation, and, since its coming into operation is postponed for several years, there seems to be no reason why this advance should not be secured without serious disorganisation of either the industry engaged in the production of the raw material or in that which utilises the finished product.

Several resolutions were adopted by the Conference, of which the most important was that submitted by the Swiss workers' delegate relating to unemployment. The Resolution was in the following terms :—

1. To instruct the International Labour Office, in conformity with the provisions of Article 396, paragraph 1, of the Treaty of Peace, to institute a special enquiry on the national and international aspects of the unemployment crisis and on the means of combating it and, whilst pursuing its enquiry with all diligence, to call into collaboration the Financial and Economic Section of the League of Nations for the solution of the financial and economic questions raised by the enquiry ;
2. To instruct the Governing Body to define the conditions, subject to which this enquiry may be made without exceeding the expenditure provided for in the budget;
3. To instruct the Governing Body to take every step within its power to secure the summoning of an international conference, which shall consider the remedies of an international character to put an end to the crisis of unemployment.

The Conference also showed its sense of the wider aspects and relations of the problem of unemployment by deciding to send a telegram to President Harding, at whose invitation the Washington Disarmament Conference was then sitting. The text of this telegram was as follows :—

The Third International Labour Conference, representing the Governments, the employers and the workers of thirty-nine nations, now in session in Geneva, greets the President of the United States on the eve of the Conference which he has convened for the limitation of armaments with deep appreciation of his great purpose and respectfully requests him to convey to the delegates assembled at Washington our most earnest wishes for the success of their deliberations. Being gathered here to seek the promotion of better social and economic conditions through international co-operation, every delegate here trusts that by the same methods the Washington Conference may achieve solid and lasting work for the firmer establishment of peace in the world, without which social stability and economic progress cannot be realised. They are convinced that the meeting of the representatives of the great American Republic with those of other great peoples from East and West cannot but materially advance the cause of humanity. May their work prosper.

It was fitting that the Conference, after dealing in a workmanlike fashion with intricate questions in the sphere of labour legislation, should lift its eyes at the close and give evidence to the world that they were not blind to the universal and recurrent problems of unemployment in its labyrinth of causes and effects.

## THE 1922 SESSION.

The 1922 Conference was a sabbatical Conference. Though only three Sessions had been held, the need for a breathing space was as much felt as if 1922 had been the Seventh Year. There was general agreement that it would be useful to hold a Conference which would take stock of the progress accomplished and in a spirit of introspection and self-examination consider problems both of general policy and of administrative machinery. This view was confirmed by the feeling which was widely entertained that the Conference had perhaps been proceeding too rapidly on the path of social reform. The six Draft Conventions and six Recommendations of Washington, the three Draft Conventions and four Recommendations of

Genoa, the seven Draft Conventions and eight Recommendations of Geneva, constituted a total of thirty-four decisions to be submitted to the legislative authorities of the world in a period of three years. Clear evidence had been given that this was more than such authorities, overwhelmed with the difficulties of the post-War period, could possibly digest. Therefore, even the States in which the interest in social reform was still strong, hailed with undisguised satisfaction the prospect of a Conference which would add but one legislative decision to the existing formidable total.

Apart from questions of internal reform, the only item on the Agenda of the 1922 Conference was " The communication to the International Labour Office of statistical and other information regarding emigration and immigration, and the repatriation and transit of emigrants." On such a subject the passions of even the most Southern delegates could hardly be expected to flare.

The President of the Conference was again Viscount Burnham. Instead of the three Vice-Presidents, who are normally chosen to assist the President, only one was appointed, owing to an interesting difficulty, due to the fact that both the employers' and the workers' delegates nominated as Vice-Presidents a delegate of France. According to the Standing Orders, the Vice-Presidents must be of different nationality, and as neither party would give way, it was finally decided that only one Vice-President should be appointed, namely, Dr. Aristides de Agüero y Bethencourt, the Government delegate of Cuba.

The difficulty which had occurred led the Conference to revise the Standing Orders so as to prevent the recurrence of a similar incident.

*International Migration Statistics.*—On the question of migration statistics, a Recommendation was unanimously adopted asking for the communication to the International Labour Office, so far as possible quarterly and within the quarter following that to which it refers, of all information available concerning emigration, immigration, repatriation and transit of emigrants, and concerning measures taken or contemplated in connection with these questions.

Secondly, Governments are asked to make every effort to communicate to the Office yearly, within six months from the end of the year, " so far as information is available," the total of their emigrants and immigrants, classified as nationals and aliens, with indications for the former and, if possible, for the latter also, of sex, age, occupation, nationality, country of last residence and country of proposed residence. Some delegates would obviously have wished to have asked for more detailed information. The women delegates particularly were concerned to make the statistics useful in connection with the work of the League of Nations in the matter of the traffic in women and children—a work in which the International Labour Office collaborates—and to this end an amendment was moved asking the Governments to observe a uniform classification as to age. The Conference, however, maintained the Commission's text, but adopted a resolution instructing the Office " to make every effort to facilitate the international co-ordination of migration statistics," and calling particularly to the attention of the Office the importance of an age classification.[1]

Thirdly, the Recommendation urges upon the Members of the Organisation the conclusion of agreements among themselves providing for the adoption of a uniform definition of the term " emigrant," the determination of uniform particulars to be entered upon the identity papers issued to emigrants and immigrants, and the use of a uniform method of recording the statistics of migration.

The importance of this Recommendation resides in the fact that it will provide the basis for future work of the Conference in dealing with problems of migration. When the International Emigration Commission appointed by the Office adopted twenty-nine

[1] The classification suggested was : Under 15 ; 15 and under 25 ; 25 to 55 ; over 55 years.

resolutions dealing with various phases of the problem of migration, emphasis was laid on the fundamental and primary importance of accurate statistical and other information. The International Labour Conference, in adopting this Recommendation, therefore took the first step with a view to future international action on a more extended scale to deal with this increasingly important problem.

*Unemployment.*—Though emigration was the only subject on the Agenda of the Conference requiring a legislative decision of the Conference, an important discussion took place on the question of unemployment. A special report on the subject was presented by the Director to the Conference in pursuance of a resolution of the Third Session which, it will be remembered, had instructed the Office to institute an enquiry and to undertake the necessary negotiations for the summoning of an international conference to study remedies of an international character for dealing with the unemployment crisis. This International Conference was not, in fact, convoked, mainly because of the holding of the International Economic Conference at Genoa under the auspices of the Supreme Council.

The Governing Body of the Office, anticipating that the Genoa Conference would be largely occupied with questions affecting unemployment, decided to co-operate as fully as possible, and at the invitation of the Italian Government, sent a delegation. Although the Genoa Economic Conference was a failure, and in any case was more largely occupied with Russia than with unemployment, it called the attention of Governments to the importance of the Conventions and Recommendations previously adopted by the International Labour Conference and recommended a number of measures that are in agreement with the provisions of those decisions. While, therefore, it was not thought necessary to convene a special Unemployment Conference, the Office continued its enquiry, and this was duly communicated to the Conference.

In the Conference discussion was concentrated largely

on the scope of the enquiry. It was felt that it was not sufficient to study merely the features of normal unemployment, but that it would be necessary to examine also the causes which led to great cyclical movements of trade and also the special causes which in the post-War world have aggravated unemployment beyond all precedent. It therefore appeared clear to the Conference that such matters as financial questions, the movement of capital, the fluctuations of exchanges as factors in the unemployment problem, should be considered in the enquiry. It was equally clear, however, to the Conference that such questions are not fully within the competence of the Organisation.

It was therefore decided that the Office should collaborate with the Economic and Financial Section of the League of Nations in the study of these aspects of the question, in order that together they might be able to contribute something to the understanding of this greatest of all social evils, which afflicts not only the worker and the employer, but the State in all its relations.

*Constitutional Reforms.*—For the rest, the Conference was almost exclusively occupied with questions of constitutional reform. It dealt with the reform of the Governing Body, the periodicity of the Sessions of the Conference, the amendment of the Standing Orders of the Conference, and the procedure of amendment of Conventions. All of these matters involve questions of great interest and difficulty with which the Organisation has been concerned on other occasions, and it has seemed best to explain the importance of each in its proper place in the final chapter, " Problems of the Present and the Future."

In a real sense the Conference was one of *recueillement*. Delegates companied together in a spirit of friendly co-operation. The machinery of the Organisation was thoroughly overhauled, not in a spirit of captious criticism, but with a genuine desire to render it more suited to cope with future difficulties, and those who laboured as fitters and turners on the

9

adjustment of frictional points were all craftsmen convinced of the value for industrial peace of the machinery to which their work was devoted.

## THE 1923 SESSION.

It had been intended that the 1923 Session should be a normal Conference, and the Agenda, as originally decided upon, comprised a number of items. A change of plan, however, took place, due to two circumstances. In the first place, demands for economy in expenditure led to the proposal that the 1923 Session of the Conference should be abandoned altogether. In the second place, one of the Governments had proposed that the normal time at which the Sessions of the Conference were held should be changed from the autumn to the spring. The Governing Body attempted to meet both suggestions, and in the end a compromise was reached according to which a short conference should be held in October 1923, and the Sixth Session of normal length in the spring of 1924. A single subject, The General Principles for the Organisation of Factory Inspection, was therefore selected from the agenda already agreed upon, and it was decided to confine the Conference of 1923 exclusively to the examination of this question. The problem, while uncontroversial, is of primordial importance for the Organisation. The decisions of the successive Sessions of the Conference are rapidly constituting an international code of labour legislation. This international code is gradually being enacted in the national legislation of the various States. But an international code, however perfect, is of no avail unless it is effectively enforced. It was therefore the question of effectively enforcing the legislative measures already taken as a result of earlier Sessions of the Conference, and to be taken as a result of Sessions still to come, which engaged the attention of the 1923 Session.

Under the circumstances it would not have been surprising if the number of States represented at the Conference had been smaller than usual. In fact, however, 42 out of the 57 States Members of the Organisation sent delegations—a larger number than at any of the preceding conferences. This is a striking indication of the real importance attached to the question by the States Members, and is an earnest that action will be taken by them in accordance with the Recommendation adopted. The delegations of these 42 countries included 74 Government delegates, 24 employers' and 24 workers' delegates, and some 70 technical advisers. As President of the Conference, M. Adatci, the first Government delegate of Japan, was elected. The Vice-Presidents were M. Pfister, one of the Swiss Government delegates ; M. Jouhaux, the French workers' representative, and M. Olivetti, a representative of the Italian employers.

Five Commissions were appointed to consider the draft resolution prepared by the Office, and after a rapid but workmanlike examination and discussion of the various phases of the problem, a comprehensive Recommendation was unanimously adopted by the Conference. The Recommendation is divided into four parts : (1) Sphere of Inspection ; (2) Nature of the Functions and Powers of Inspectors ; (3) Organisation of Inspection, and (4) Inspectors' Reports.

(1) The Recommendation lays down that it should be the principal function of the system of inspection to secure the enforcement of the laws and regulations relating to the conditions of work and the protection of the workers while engaged in their work (hours of work and rest, night work, prohibition of the employment of certain persons on dangerous, unhealthy or physically unsuitable work, health and safety, etc.). A general provision is also added to the effect that inspectors may be assigned additional duties, which may vary according to the conception of the traditions and customs prevailing in the different countries.

(2) The section with regard to the nature of the functions and powers of inspectors lays down that inspectors provided with credentials should be empowered by law :—

(a) To visit and inspect, at any hour of the day or night, places where they may have reasonable cause to believe that persons under the protection of the law are employed, and to enter by day any place which they may have reasonable cause to believe to be an establishment, or part thereof, subject to their supervision; provided that, before leaving, inspectors should, if possible, notify the employer or some representative of the employer of their visit ;

(b) To question, without witnesses, the staff belonging to the establishment, and, for the purpose of carrying out their duties, to apply for information to any other persons whose evidence they may consider necessary, and to require to be shown any registers or documents which the laws regulating conditions of work require to be kept.

Some discussion took place on the question of giving inspectors power to bring breaches of the law directly before the competent judicial authorities. The debate revealed a divergence between the Anglo-Saxon and the continental systems, the principle of the former being to maintain a clear division between the administrative and judicial authorities, whereas the continental principle tends to favour the extension of the powers of the inspector. The Recommendation therefore provides that inspectors should be empowered to bring breaches of the laws directly before the competent judicial authorities, regard being had to the administrative and judicial systems of each country, and subject to such reference to superior authority as may be considered necessary.

Detailed provisions are laid down with regard to safety. Inspection should be increasingly directed towards securing the adoption of the most suitable safety methods for preventing accidents and diseases with a view to rendering work less dangerous, more healthy and even less exhausting. The following methods were therefore recommended :—

(a) That all accidents should be notified to the competent authorities.

(b) That inspectors should inform and advise employers respecting the best standards of health and safety.

(c) That inspectors should encourage the collaboration of employers, managing staff and workers for the promotion of personal caution, safety methods and the perfecting of safety equipment.

(*d*) That inspectors should endeavour to promote the improvement and perfecting of measures of health and safety.

(*e*) That in countries where it is considered preferable to have a special organisation for accident insurance and prevention completely independent of the inspectorate, the special officers of such organisations should be guided by the foregoing principles.

(3) The section on the organisation of inspection was subdivided into three sub-sections, relating respectively to the organisation of the staff, the qualifications and training of inspectors, the standard and methods of inspection and the co-operation of employers and workers. The Recommendation provides that the inspectors should, as far as possible, be localised, and that all inspectors in a particular district should be placed under the general supervision of an inspector of high qualifications and experience. It was further considered necessary that the inspector should be placed under the direct and exclusive control of a central State authority, and should not be under the control of, or in any way responsible to, any local authority. It was also regarded as essential that among the inspectors should be included experts having competent medical, engineering, electrical or other scientific training and experience, and also women. The Recommendation attaches importance to the provision that the inspectorate should be on a permanent basis and independent of changes of Government. It also urges that the workers and their representatives should be afforded every facility for communicating freely with the inspectors as to any defect or breach of the law in the establishment in which they are employed, and further, that inspectors should confer from time to time with the representatives of the employers' and workers' organisations.

(4) It is also recommended that inspectors should regularly submit to their central authority reports framed on uniform lines dealing with their work and its results, and that this authority should publish

an annual report.  Details are also given as to the
kinds of information to be contained in the reports
of inspectors.

Among the supplementary resolutions adopted, one
invited the Governing Body to consider the possibility
of inscribing on the Agenda of a forthcoming Session of the Conference "The institution of a special
inspection system for the mercantile marine," and
another requested the Governing Body to obtain
information from Governments and from international
technical and industrial organisations upon the question
of automatic couplings.  It was considered that this
question was of great importance for the safety of
railway workers.

That the last Conference was the most representative of the series is of importance from two points
of view.

In the first place, countries which have no system
of factory inspection, or in which the system is inadequate, have been impressed with the importance
attached by international opinion to the institution
of labour inspection and its place in modern industrial
civilisation.

In the second place, this Conference—the most
recent—is the best evidence that has ever been given
of the recognition by the States of the world of the
enduring value of the International Labour Organisation.  The Agenda contained nothing controversial,
nothing sensational.  Yet a greater number of States
than ever before thought it necessary to send delegations.  It was realised that the Conference was called
to assure the foundations of the whole of the super-
structure of international labour legislation.  The casual
passer-by pays more attention to the dome than to the
foundations, but the man who cares knows that the
foundation is everything.

# CHAPTER VII

## RESULTS OF THE CONFERENCE IN NATIONAL LEGISLATION

THE Conference would ultimately be of no value unless its results were embodied in national legislation. It does not exist to establish a theoretical standard for the national legislator to contemplate in the abstract. Its *raison d'être* is to adopt decisions capable of being embodied with the least possible delay in national legislation. The touchstone of the success of the Organisation is therefore the extent to which its decisions have been incorporated in the organised system of legislation of the various countries.

What, then, are the facts? They are summarised in the following table, which shows the position on October 1, 1922, and on October 1, 1923 :—

|  | 1922 | 1923 | *Increase* |
|---|---|---|---|
| 1. *Ratifications.* | | | |
| Ratifications communicated | 51 | 86 | 35 |
| Ratifications authorised but not yet communicated | 16 | 23 | 7 |
| Total | — | — | 42 |
| Ratifications recommended | 85 | 127 | 42 |
| 2. *Application.* | | | |
| Legislative measures adopted, introduced or prepared with a view to the application of Conventions or Recommendations | 172 | 275 | 103 |
| 3. *Legislative activity.* | | | |
| General total of measures for ratification and application | 324 | 511 | 187 |

It will be seen from this table not only that the results are considerable, but that they have shown a marked tendency to increase.

With regard to each of the main subjects on which the Conference has adopted decisions, it is of interest to consider in some detail the extent of the measures which have been adopted.

*Hours of Work.*—The Convention on Hours of Work of the Washington Conference has been ratified in only five States—Bulgaria, Czechoslovakia, Greece, India and Roumania. It will be seen that none of these States is quite in the first rank of industrial States. This fact is undoubtedly serious, and it has naturally engaged deeply the attention of the Office, of the Governing Body and of the Conference itself. The Governing Body was led to undertake a special examination of the difficulties encountered in the ratification of the Draft Convention on Hours of Labour as a result of a proposal of the British Government.

That Government, in a letter of July 22, 1921, explained that the British Government had examined the possibility of ratifying the Draft Convention, and that it found itself faced by two kinds of difficulty. The system under which hours of labour are regulated in Great Britain is by way of collective agreements. These collective agreements leave considerable freedom as a general rule with regard to the authorisation of overtime in excess of forty-eight hours in the week. Now the Draft Convention, in the opinion of the British Government, did not permit such flexibility. It was further pointed out that the agreements concluded between railway companies and the unions of railway workers authorised in excess of eight hours per day and forty-eight hours per week daily extensions of work, or Sunday work, which did not seem compatible with the terms of the Draft Convention.

The British Government therefore indicated that they considered it advisable that the whole question should be considered at a future Conference, the aim of the Conference being to adopt a new Hours Convention, retaining those provisions of the Washington Convention which had proved generally acceptable in the light of recent experience, and omitting or modifying those which might appear to be too inelastic for the varying needs of the different industries in the respective countries.

The Governing Body considered this letter at the Ninth Session. The Director indicated that the two problems raised in the letter of the British Government should be kept strictly distinct. With regard to the question of interpretation, he expressed the view of the Office that neither of the difficulties was incompatible with the terms of the Draft Convention. Dealing with the further question raised by the British Government, namely, the possibility of referring the whole question to a further Session of the Conference with a view to revision of the Draft Convention, the Director enumerated the serious objections to which, in his opinion, such a solution must give rise. In the first place, a certain number of States had already ratified the Draft Convention, and its provisions were already, owing to this fact, legally in force. In the second place, the adoption of a new Draft Convention, which might not command the quasi-unanimity secured in the Washington Convention, would not afford more effective guarantees to the International Labour Organisation. Finally, to call once more into question a reform solemnly adopted by the Washington Conference would be a serious blow to the prestige of the Organisation. The Director therefore suggested that the Governing Body should be regarded as the competent authority to give an authoritative interpretation of the text of the Convention which would offer all the necessary guarantees to the British Government.[1]

This proposal was, however, not accepted by the Governing Body. Sir Montague Barlow, on behalf of the British Government, opposed the suggestion on juridical grounds, and the Chairman of the Governing Body expressed the opinion that the Governing Body was not qualified to give a juridical interpretation of the text of the Convention. He further emphasised

---

[1] *Special Report on the Situation with regard to the Ratification of the Hours Convention*, Geneva, 1922, pp. 8–9.

the fact that if the British Government declared itself unable to regard such an interpretation as a valid one, the procedure suggested by the Director would not seem calculated to lead to a solution.

In the end, the Governing Body decided to instruct the Director to enter into communication with the Governments of countries which had experienced difficulty in ratifying the Hours Convention with a view to finding a solution of the difficulties. A long series of negotiations subsequently took place, of which the Governing Body was kept informed. In the end, a full discussion on the question took place at the meeting of the Governing Body in April 1922.

The Director had proposed that the Governing Body should decide to request Governments which had not yet ratified the Draft Convention to inform the Office what were the particular points as regards which they were encountering difficulties which prevented them from ratifying. The Conference could then examine if it was advisable to undertake with regard to certain stated points a revision of the provisions as originally adopted. After a long discussion, the Governing Body arrived at the following conclusions :—

1. That it appeared at least premature to take any action tending to a revision of the Hours Convention by the Conference;
2. That the procedure proposed by the Office did not appear to offer sufficient guarantees to the British Government, while the Governing Body, for its part, had not been of the opinion that it could constitute inself as an authority invested with judicial powers for the interpretation of Conventions;
3. That, until it was possible to take a decision, the International Labour Office was to continue, in accordance with the terms of Article 396 of the Treaty, to keep its information up to date as far as possible with a view to following the destinies of the Hours Convention, and thus enabling the Conference to form an exact opinion of the situation.

The results of the enquiries made by the Office, and the information it thus collected, were published in a special Report submitted to the Fourth Session of the Conference. The matter was further considered by the Governing

Body at its Eighteenth Session, and a Committee was appointed to make Recommendations as to the means of furthering the ratification of the Convention. The Committee, after thoroughly examining the question, recommended at the Twentieth Session that, in view of the danger and difficulty of revising the Convention, it was desirable, before taking up any question with regard to the question of revision, to request the countries which desired to ratify, but had been unable to do so, to indicate the precise nature of their difficulties and the changes which they suggested. The workers' group desired to maintain the present text as embodying the standard for the eight-hour-day system, and refused to agree to any steps which might lead even indirectly to revision. The workers' delegates accordingly opposed the recommendations of the Committee. The Governing Body finally decided to take no action.

This may appear to be a disappointing result of these long discussions. But have the discussions been entirely valueless? Has the information that has been collected been amassed in vain? Only history can say.[1] At the least, however, the discussion has served to keep before public opinion the enormous importance of the question of the Eight-Hour Day. In many countries, indeed, the principle of the eight-hour day is at present being strongly attacked, either on grounds of the danger of foreign competition, or because of the reduction in output which is, or is supposed to be, a result of the eight-hour-day rule. The fact, however, which emerges from a study of the information objectively collected by the International Labour Office, is that there exists practically no country where, since 1918, the eight-hour day has not been accepted as the common rule. Even where it has been criticised, even where anxiety has been manifested by employers

[1] Since the above was written, events have moved rapidly, in various countries, in favour of the maintenance of the eight hour day. During the month of February 1924, decisions have been taken, or official announcements made, in this sense in Austria, Belgium, Poland and Switzerland. On 27 February in the British House of Commons the Minister of Labour announced that he proposed to introduce legislation at an early date dealing with the Hours Convention.

or by the Government, even where special exceptions
have appeared indispensable, the eight-hour day remains
at the present time in force in most of the great
industrial countries of the world.

*Unemployment.*—If States have been slow to give
effect to the decision of the Conference with regard to
Hours of Labour, they have lost little time in ratifying
the Conventions relating to Unemployment. The
Washington Draft Convention relating to the establishment of free employment exchanges has been ratified
by the following countries : Bulgaria, Denmark,
Esthonia, Finland, Great Britain, Greece, India, Italy,
Japan, Norway, Roumania, Spain, Sweden, Switzerland—
while the Genoa Draft Convention on facilities for finding employment for seamen has been ratified by
Bulgaria, Esthonia, Finland, Japan, Norway, Sweden.
Measures have also been taken in various countries
to apply the Draft Convention on Unemployment Indemnity in the case of loss or foundering of the ship,
the Recommendation on Unemployment Insurance, and
the Recommendation on Unemployment in Agriculture.

*Conditions of Work of Women and Children.*—A
large number of States have also ratified the decisions
of the Conference relating to the employment of women.
The Draft Convention on the night work of women has
been ratified by Bulgaria, Czechoslovakia, Esthonia,
Great Britain, Greece, India, Italy, the Netherlands,
Roumania, South Africa and Switzerland, and the Draft
Convention relating to maternity by Bulgaria, Greece,
Roumania and Spain.

Even greater results have been obtained in connection with the Draft Conventions relating to the
conditions of work of children and young persons.
The Washington Draft Convention on the minimum
age for the employment of children has been ratified
by Bulgaria, Czechoslovakia, Denmark, Esthonia, Great
Britain, Greece, Roumania and Switzerland, and the
Draft Convention of the Genoa Conference on the minimum age for the employment of young persons at sea
has been ratified by Bulgaria, Esthonia, Great Britain,

Roumania and Sweden. Certain States have also ratified the Draft Conventions of the Geneva Conference concerning the age of admission to agriculture and concerning the age of admission to work as trimmers and stokers. The Washington Draft Convention, with regard to the night work of young persons, has been ratified by Bulgaria, Denmark, Esthonia, Great Britain, Greece, India, Italy, Roumania and Switzerland.

Full details with regard to the States which have ratified the Conventions, and the measures which they have taken to apply them in national legislation, are regularly published by the International Labour Office. The details are too numerous to reproduce here. It should, however, be mentioned that in Great Britain effect was given to the decisions of the International Labour Conference on these questions by two Acts : the Women, Young Persons and Children (Employment) Act, 1920, and the Women and Young Persons (Employment in Lead Processes) Act, 1920. The first of these Acts brings British law into conformity with the Washington Conventions on the minimum age for the admission of children to employment, the night work of young persons, and the night work of women, and with the Genoa Convention on the minimum age for the admission of children to employment at sea. It should be noted that this Act abolished half-time work of children in Great Britain. The second Act gives effect to the Recommendation of the Washington Conference concerning the protection of women and children against lead poisoning.

*Eastern Countries.*—Special interest attaches to the measures which have been taken in Eastern countries to give effect to the decisions of the Conference. It was anticipated at the Peace Conference that it would be relatively easy to secure standardisation of conditions in European countries, but extremely difficult to obtain this in Oriental countries. Owing, however, to the economic disorganisation of Europe resulting from the War, experience has been contrary to anticipation. The most interesting and, in some ways, the most important results of the work of the Organisation are to be seen in the East rather than in Europe.

It was not, of course, intended that conditions in Eastern countries should at a single leap be raised to the same level as those obtaining in European countries. The Peace Treaty explicitly laid down that in framing any Recommendation or Draft Convention, " the Conference shall have due regard to those countries in which climatic conditions, the imperfect development of industrial organisation, or other special circumstances, make the industrial conditions substantially different." It would clearly be useless to wish to apply automatically to China or Siam Conventions framed to fit the economic conditions of France or Great Britain. Therefore, in drafting Conventions and Recommendations, the policy has been followed of granting exceptions for special methods of application in the countries of backward development, with provision for investigations and reports with a view to promoting a gradual elevation of the standard. In no country have the decisions of the International Labour Conference led to greater immediate results than in India.

The Washington Conference laid down that in the case of India an exceptional régime, based on a sixty-hour week, should apply. This exceptional régime was applicable to all workers in industries then covered by the Factory Acts, in mines and in certain branches of railway work. At the same time, the Commission on Special Countries proposed that the Conference should lay before the Government of India a very urgent request that it should consider two important matters—first, the possibility of adopting a lower limit for underground work in mines, and secondly, the possibility of adopting a modified definition of " factory " which would reduce the number of workers required to bring a factory under the scope of the Act.

The Government of India duly considered these proposals and, as a result, the sixty-hour week has been introduced and the Indian Factories Act has been modified. The Indian Government took the opportunity at the same time to insert in the Act a certain number of other reforms resulting from the decisions of the Washington Conference. Under the old Factories Act, only factories employing not less than fifty persons and using mechanical power were included among industrial undertakings. Under the new Act, the term " factory " is applied in all cases where twenty workers are employed, and the local Governments are authorised to include under the term " factory " undertakings employing only ten persons, whether these undertakings use mechanical power or not. The adoption of this Act consequently constituted very considerable progress, both in legislation and in practice.

Other measures have been adopted by the Indian Government with a view to applying the decisions of the Conference, notably those relating to the work of women and to the work of children.

Thus India has raised the minimum age for the employment of children from nine years to twelve years and has reduced the number of hours during which a child may be employed in a factory from seven to six per day. It has also ratified the Unemployment Convention of the Washington Conference providing *inter alia* for the establishment of free public employment exchanges and for reciprocity of treatment for immigrants under unemployment insurance systems. Among other legislative measures adopted in accordance with the Conventions and Recommendations of the International Labour Conference, mention may be made of the fact that India has adhered to the Berne Convention of 1906 prohibiting the use of white phosphorus in the manufacture of matches.

The action taken by India with regard to the ratification of these Conventions may be considered as the first tangible results in the East of the ideals inspired by Part XIII of the Treaty. In India, in fact, a vast social revolution has been realised which will have a far-reaching effect in leading to the world-wide equilibrium in social conditions which is one of the aims of the International Labour Organisation.

Japan has also taken a prominent position among the States which have given effect to the decisions of the International Labour Conference. This country has prohibited the employment of children under the age of twelve and stipulated that children over the age of twelve may only be admitted to employment if they have finished the elementary school course. Japan has also prohibited the employment on board ship of children under the age of fourteen, and the employment of any child or young person under eighteen years of age unless he is provided with a medical certificate attesting fitness for such work. Legislation has also been adopted embodying general principles for the protection of women before and after childbirth, and a further Act has been passed providing that the night work of women and young persons should be absolutely prohibited three years from the date of the enforcement of the Act. Japan has also given effect to the Unemployment Convention of the Washington Conference and it has adhered to the Berne Convention of 1906 prohibiting the use of white phosphorus in the manufacture of matches.

The various provisions enumerated above are included in the following Acts : Unemployment Exchange Act of 1921; Employment of Seamen Act, 1922 ; Prohibition of White Phosphorus Act, 1921; Factory Act Amendment Act, 1923; Minimum Age of Industrial Workers Act, 1923 ; Minimum Age and Health Certificate of Seamen Act, 1923. This mass of legislation, again inspired in all its details by the Draft Conventions and Recommendations of the International Labour Conference, amounts to the inauguration of a completely new system of labour legislation in Japan.

In the case of China, the Washington Conference decided that the country should be exempted from the scope of the Draft Convention on Hours of Labour. Nevertheless, the Commission on Special Countries of that Conference attached great importance to the acceptance by the Chinese Government of the principle of the protection of labour by factory legislation. It recognised that China was still very largely an undeveloped country, and that it was faced with special difficulties such as the vast extent of its territory, the fact that the Government did not possess tariff autonomy, and the existence of foreign settlements and leased territories, which, combined with the lack of experience in factory legislation, made it impossible for China immediately to conform to Western standards. It therefore suggested that the Government should consider the possibility of adopting a Convention embodying the principle of a ten-hour day or a sixty-hour week for adult workers, and an eight-hour day or a forty-eight-hour week for workers under fifteen years of age, and that the Convention should also embody the principle of a weekly rest-day. The Commission also proposed that all factories employing over one hundred workers should come within the scope of the suggested legislation.

The Chinese Government, after considerable delay, gave effect in March 1923 to the essential points of the proposals of the Commission. These were included in a Presidential Decree promulgating Provisional Factory Regulations prepared by the Minister of Agriculture and Commerce.

Two other countries call for special mention. These are Persia and Siam. No information has, as a matter of fact, been furnished by these countries to the Office concerning the steps which they propose to take to ratify the Conventions. As, however, industrial development continues to increase in these countries as in the rest of the East, they will no doubt experience the desirability of bringing themselves into line with those States which are progressively attempting to adapt their legislation to the standards of the more advanced countries.

It was by a happy historical conjuncture that the emergence into life of a new social conscience in the countries of the East coincided with the creation of the International Labour Organisation.

# CHAPTER VIII

## INTERNATIONAL COMMISSIONS

MOST valuable assistance has been given to the International Labour Office by the various International Commissions which have been appointed at various periods during the last four years. In some national administrations it has become a habit, if some question grows particularly troublesome, to refer it to a Commission in the hope that it will become so buried under masses of reports that the only subsequent action required is a decent interment. This has not been the policy of the International Labour Office. Its Commissions have in all cases been set up because there was some special piece of work that could only be done with their assistance.

The kinds of work to be done by the Commissions have varied considerably, and the immediate objects of their establishment have also been diverse. In some cases they were set up to respond to the resolutions of the Conferences; in others to assist the scientific studies of one of the Sections of the Office; in others to meet a need felt by a number of persons interested in a certain problems; in other cases again to secure within the Office a more direct representation of certain interests.

The various Commissions fall into four groups. The first class consists of standing representative commissions. These are permanent Standing Commissions, whose composition is determined by the Governing Body, and whose members are appointed by it. Such Commissions are representative of the three sides of the international labour triangle. To some extent they are a reflection of the constitution of the Governing Body itself. The Governing Body fixes their agenda and the dates of their sessions, and the proposals or resolutions they adopt are submitted for approval to the Governing Body. The main object of such Standing Representative Commissions is to secure within the Organisation bodies capable of discussing with full technical knowledge and experience some of the special problems with which the Organisation is called upon to deal.

The second class of Commission is similar to the first category, with this exception, that it is not representative solely of the Organisation, but involves the collaboration of another institution. On such a Commission both organisations are represented equally, and their task is to discuss and reach agreement on matters which to some extent concern both organisations. At present there is only one example of such a Commission, namely, the Mixed Agricultural Commission. There can be little doubt, however, that in the future more of these Commissions will be appointed in order to deal with rapidity and authority with the questions which are not exclusively the resort of the International Labour Organisation, but in which, nevertheless, it has a real interest.

Into the third class of Commission fall certain *ad hoc* Commissions. These Commissions have been established for some definite purpose, and when the determinate questions for which they have been called into being have been reported on by them, they cease to exist. Such Commissions may be compared to the Royal Commissions set up in Great Britain to deal with some specific subject once and for all.

The fourth class it is perhaps hardly accurate to call Commissions at all. Strictly speaking, they are conferences of experts who have been invited by the Office to assist in the scientific work executed by its different services. Representatives of organisations or of industrial associations or of groups bound by some common tie may participate in such conferences. But the men who are lent by these organisations attend the conferences solely in the capacity of experts. The Governing Body has deemed it possible to leave to the Director the responsibility for the scientific work of the Office and for deciding at what time and on what point consultations of experts shall be held. It has, furthermore, been decided that all experts on certain matters may be regarded as forming internationally a kind of large Correspondence Committee, the members of which are summoned to special conferences only if the need becomes clearly evident.

## I. REPRESENTATIVE STANDING COMMISSIONS.

The first Representative Standing Commission to be established, and also the most important, was the Joint Maritime Commission. The creation of this Commission was decided upon by the Governing Body of the International Labour Office during its Third Session in March 1920. It is of some interest to bear in mind the motives which led to its establishment. Maritime labour involves conditions of so special a character that, when the Peace Treaty was being drafted, the seamen claimed the creation of a special office of maritime labour. The Peace Conference considered it necessary to take account of their request to the extent, at any rate, of arranging for the convocation of a special conference. The Commission on International Labour Legislation of the Peace Conference adopted a resolution in this sense.

The Governing Body therefore considered it one of its first duties to respond to this appeal, and decided that a Joint Commission would facilitate the work of the International Labour Organisation in the examination of problems relating to maritime labour, and would probably, to a considerable extent, meet the desires of the seamen.

The Governing Body determined that the Commission should include five shipowners and five seamen, to be appointed by the Genoa Conference, together with two members elected by the Governing Body of the Office. It was further decided that the Commission should be consulted on all questions relating to maritime labour. The Genoa Conference approved the nominations submitted to it by the groups of shipowners and seamen respectively, and granted the seats of the shipowners to Belgium, Canada, Great Britain, Japan and Sweden, and those of the seamen to France, Germany, Great Britain, Italy and Norway.

During its Fifth Session, held at Geneva in October 1920, the Governing Body completed the composition of this Commission by appointing the two members to be elected from its midst, namely, the representative of the French employers, M. Pinot, and the representative of the Dutch workers, M. Oudegeest.

During the 1921 Session of the International Labour Conference, a resolution was adopted defining more clearly and, at the same time, extending the duties of the Commission. It provided in the first place that measures of protection adopted in favour of the general body of workers should not be applied automatically to workers in the mercantile marine and, in the second place, that all questions of a maritime nature submitted to the examination of the Conference should be brought beforehand before the Joint Maritime Commission for study. The Geneva Conference thus showed clearly its intention not only of making questions of maritime labour the subject of special decisions, but of making compulsory the consultation of the Joint Maritime Commission on all questions within the sphere of the International Labour Organisation which, directly or indirectly, might be of interest to the mercantile marine.

The First Session of the Joint Maritime Commission was held at Geneva from November 8–10, 1920, under the chairmanship of M. Arthur Fontaine. The two principal items on the Agenda were the discussions of the decisions of the Genoa Conference, which involved action on the part of the Commission, and questions relating to the establishment of an international seamen's code.

The Second Session of the Commission, held in Paris, March 7–8, 1922, under the chairmanship of M. Arthur Fontaine, discussed the following Agenda : Study of conditions of work in the fishing industry; social insurance; deck cargoes ; unemployment insurance for seamen; hours of work in the mercantile marine ; international seamen's code.

As a result of these two meetings of the Joint Maritime Commission, definite action has been taken on more than one question.  The manner in which the Genoa Conference envisaged the preparation of an international seamen's code has already been explained.  The Maritime Commission, giving effect to the general lines of the decision of the Genoa Conference, decided to ask the Office to ascertain from Governments the measures taken or contemplated by them for the establishment of national codes as required by the Genoa Conference—further, to send to the Governments, and also to the national shipowners' and seamen's organisations for their observations, a memorandum on the methods adopted for the preparation of an international code, and finally, to draw up, as a preliminary measure, a scheme for the international codification of seamen's articles of agreement.  In accordance with this decision, the Office prepared and sent to the Governments of States Members of the Organisation, under the title of the " International Seamen's Code," a publication giving a history of the question and a questionnaire containing detailed questions to which Governments were asked to reply.  A large number of replies to the questionnaire were received from Governments, and in accordance with the suggestion of the Joint Maritime Commission, M. Ripert, Professor of the Faculty of Law and of the School of Political Science, Paris, has been entrusted with the preparation of a draft code.  As soon as this initial work is completed the draft will be submitted to the Joint Maritime Commission for its observations.  The procedure then to be taken will consist in its reference to the Governing Body, which will decide whether it considers it possible to submit it to Governments with a view to adoption by a Conference.  The Joint Maritime Commission has fully shared the view expressed by the Genoa Conference itself, that on such a matter it is necessary to proceed with great deliberation in view of the fact that if such a code is to be definitely established, it will form the foundation of international maritime law, so far as conditions of labour are concerned, for a very long period of time.

A further important question dealt with by the Joint Maritime Commission was the protection of the health of seamen. On this matter again, the discussions of the Joint Maritime Commission derived directly from the Genoa Conference. That Conference adopted a resolution to the effect that the Health Section of the League of Nations should consider the following questions :—

1. The provision of adequate facilities for the prevention and treatment of venereal diseases at all the principal ports.
2. The inclusion of venereal diseases under the conditions for which free drugs and treatment are provided for members of the Mercantile Marine.
3. The dissemination of appropriate information on the subject to seafarers, and especially to those at training establishments.
4. The provision of adequate facilities for recreation at all large ports, under the administration of joint organisations, representative of owners and seamen.

In accordance with this resolution, the Office approached the Secretary-General of the League of Nations with a view to arranging collaboration with it. The Secretary-General was of opinion that the question of venereal disease, in so far as it relates to the work of the mercantile marine, was largely the concern of the International Labour Office, and considered that the question should be studied jointly by the Health Organisation of the League of Nations and the Industrial Hygiene Service of the International Labour Office.

The Director then consulted the Joint Maritime Commission with regard to the programme to be followed. During its First Session the Commission authorised the Office to proceed to an enquiry into the measures to be taken with a view to facilitating the prevention and treatment of venereal diseases at large seaports, and to include the disease amongst those for which treatment and drugs are supplied free of charge to men in the mercantile marine. The Commission also emphasised the desirability of an immediate campaign of propaganda amongst seamen's organisations by bringing the importance of the matter to the attention of Governments. In accordance with this decision, the Office communicated with Governments, and from several of them replies have been received indicating the steps which they could take or envisage in connection with this matter.

The Office has also been engaged in the consideration of the possibility of preparing a Draft Convention on the prevention or treatment of venereal diseases among seamen. With this object, it sought the co-operation of the International Office of Public Hygiene and the Health Committee of the League of Nations. The International Office of Public Hygiene has already prepared a Draft Convention on the treatment of venereal diseases. The transmission to Governments of this Draft by the Office had been considered, but it was in the end decided that the International Office of Public Hygiene should in the first place submit it as a suggestion to the Governments signatories of the Rome Convention of December 9, 1907, by which the Office was established.

The Health Committee of the League of Nations has considered the problem of the standardisation of serums, and an International Conference on the subject was held in London in December 1921. A sub-Committee of the Conference was specially entrusted with the sero-diagnosis of syphilis. It is understood that the work of this sub-Committee has been delayed by serious technical difficulties.

In view of this, the Office has considered that the organisation of the campaign against venereal diseases among seamen should not necessarily be bound up with the problem of methods of treatment. It has therefore prepared a brochure, which will bring together all the available information and will give an account of the present position of the problem and of the solutions which appear possible.  A questionnaire will be annexed to this brochure with a view to an enquiry among Governments and organisations on the attitude which they adopt towards an international Draft Convention on the question.

Among other subjects on which the Joint Maritime Commission took decisions figure the question of unemployment insurance for seamen, the conditions of work in the fishing industry, the regulation of deck cargoes, and the conditions of social insurance for seamen.

Perhaps the most important question which engaged the attention of the Joint Maritime Commission has been the question of the regulation of hours of work on board ship.  It will be remembered that the Genoa Conference failed to adopt a Draft Convention providing for an eight-hour day on board ship, and it fell to the Joint Maritime Commission to continue negotiations with regard to the matter.  At its First Session, the Joint Maritime Commission was asked to decide whether it considered that the Draft Convention should be communicated to the Governments according to the procedure laid down in Article 407 of the Peace Treaty, which provides that if any Convention coming before the Conference fails to secure the support of two-thirds of the votes cast by the delegates present, it shall nevertheless be within the right of any members of the permanent Organisation to agree to such a Convention among themselves.  The Joint Maritime Commission considered that no action of this kind should be taken until the negotiations which had been proposed between the International Shipowners' Federation and the International Seafarers' Federation were concluded.

In accordance with the suggestion of the Commission, a Conference was held at Brussels in January 1921 between representatives of these two organisations.  The Chair was taken by the Director of the International Labour Office.  It was decided that the technical details of the application of a shorter working day should be discussed by two committees, one dealing with deck and engine-room hands, and the other with the general services. The former Committee held several meetings in London, but the second did not meet. Negotiations were in the end discontinued.

The Joint Maritime Commission, at its Second Session, was informed of the situation, and asked to state what steps could be taken in order to find some means of coming to an agreement on the question of hours of work. The seamen's representative urged that negotiations should be resumed, and that efforts should be made for the application in the principal maritime countries of the eight-hour day, which was already in force in the French mercantile marine. The shipowners' representatives stated that owing to the critical situation of maritime transport and of economic conditions which were beyond their control, they could not then contemplate any reduction in the working hours of seamen. After some discussion it was decided, however, that negotiations should not be definitely broken off, and it was agreed that a further meeting to discuss the question should be held. The Commission requested the International Labour Office in the meantime to continue to study the question and to attempt to find a basis on which negotiations could be carried on.

*Commission on Unemployment.*—During its meeting of June 9, 1920, the Governing Body decided to establish a Commission of three members, one chosen from each of the three groups represented on the Governing Body. The creation of this Commission took place in accordance with the resolution adopted by the Washington Conference, inviting the Governing Body to constitute an International Commission " empowered to formulate recommendations upon the best methods to be adopted in each State for collecting and publishing all information relative to the problem of unemployment, in such form and for such periods of time as may be internationally comparable."

The Commission on Unemployment met for the first time at Geneva on October 7, 1920, under the chairmanship of M. Oudegeest. It studied a report which

had been prepared by the technical service for unemployment and emigration.  As several of the questions raised
were of a purely technical nature, the report proposed
to appoint experts to discuss the conclusions relative to
the matter.  The Commission accordingly decided to
invite a certain number of experts to a meeting to
be held in Paris, and to submit to them the scheme
of work drawn up by the services of the Office.  In
accordance with this decision, the Commission met again
in Paris on November 30 and December 1, 1920, to
hear the experts who had been appointed : Sir William
Beveridge (London), Mm. Max Lazard (Paris), Lucien
March (Paris), H. W. Methorst (The Hague), Ricci
(Rome), N. Rygg (Christiania), Weigert (Berlin).

The experts recognised that it would be necessary for
the international comparison of statistics, and for the
deduction from them of useful information in the
campaign against unemployment, to publish them in
as detailed a form as possible for each industry and
trade, and to establish for this purpose a classified
list of industries and trades as agreed upon by the
various countries.  The problem of the definition of
unemployment was also investigated, and it was considered necessary that the various countries should arrive
at a common definition which would ultimately be differentiated according to the industries concerned.  The
experts undertook to develop their statements in the
form of written memoranda, which would be submitted
to the Commission at a subsequent meeting.

On January 10–11, 1921, the Commission again met
at Geneva to examine the written communications
furnished by the experts.  The Commission decided
first of all to carry out the work of establishing an
international classification of industries and trades to
be submitted to the Governments of the Members of
the International Labour Organisation in order that
they might publish their unemployment statistics in
parallel form, and instructed the technical unemployment
service to prepare this work for the following session.

That session was held at Geneva on April 11, 1921.

After having studied the classified lists of industries and trades adopted by the French Labour Ministry, the Commission decided to propose to the Governing Body that this classification with certain amendments should be submitted to the Governments of the Members of the International Labour Organisation for their consideration.

The Commission also adopted a definition of involuntary unemployment for submission to the Governments, and finally decided that it would be desirable to consult the latter in the matter of the drawing up of uniform model schedules on which the unemployment statistics collected by trade unions and employment agencies would periodically figure. The proposal of the Unemployment Commission to submit these draft proposals to the Governments for observations was approved by the Governing Body of the International Labour Office during its Seventh Session, held at Geneva from April 12–14, 1921.

The draft proposals of the Unemployment Commission were duly submitted to the Governments. A Report is being prepared by the Commission for submission to the Governing Body, including the suggestions made by the Governments.

On this question also the Office has been impressed with the necessity of moving with deliberation. The extent to which the world has suffered under the terrible scourge of unemployment during recent years has, it is true, constituted a temptation to embark upon hasty proposals. The Office has felt, however, that any momentary advantage that might possibly accrue from such a course would be more than counterbalanced by the weaknesses which would almost inevitably be involved in any scheme adopted without the most mature deliberation.

II. REPRESENTATIVE STANDING JOINT COMMISSIONS.

There is at present in existence only one Commission belonging to this class—that is, the Mixed Advisory Committee on Agriculture. The steps which led to the establishment of this Committee are interesting, particularly as illustrating the difficulties that arise in reaching agreement on the constitution of committees appointed to deal with industries whose organisation is complicated, and representing two organisations, each of which are from one aspect concerned with conditions in the industry. When agricultural questions were for the first time placed on the Agenda of a Session of the Conference, the Director considered the desirability of proposing to set up a Joint Agricultural Commission formed on lines similar to those of the Joint Maritime Commission. In the case of both agricultural labour and seafaring labour conditions are peculiar, and it was therefore considered desirable that the Organisation should obtain the assistance of experienced persons particularly qualified in agriculture. This view was also shared by the 1921 Conference, which decided to submit certain questions to a Joint Agricultural Commission formed in a similar manner to the Joint Maritime Commission. The establishment of this Commission was, however, delayed by two difficulties. The first difficulty was that there was already in existence another institution which dealt with questions of agriculture. This is the International Institute of Agriculture which, while it treats more particularly questions of agricultural production, might be considered, in virtue of certain clauses in its constitution which give it the right to deal with questions of agricultural labour, to desire to consider also problems of the regulation of labour. There was therefore a fear that the work of the two institutions would be needlessly duplicated. In view of the possibility of conflicts of jurisdiction between the two organisations, it appeared important to avoid them in advance through loyal collaboration. Further, at this time (January 1922), the whole question of the competence of the Organisation in agricultural matters had been submitted to the decision of the Permanent Court of International Justice at The Hague.

In view of these two facts, it was decided to adjourn the appointment of the Commission, but in the meantime the Governing Body invited the Director to examine the possibility of collaborating with the International Institute of Agriculture. In accordance with this decision, the Director entered into communication with the Institute, and a meeting took place in June 1922 of a Mixed Committee of the Governing Body and the International Institute of Agriculture. This Committee found itself, after a complete exchange of views, in full agreement on all the questions discussed, and proposed the institution of a Mixed Committee composed of three representatives of each of the two institutions. In making these proposals, the Joint Committee took into consideration the special difficulties that were involved.

In agriculture, organisations of employers and workers are hardly comparable with similar organisations in manufacturing industry. In addition to employers as such and wage-earning workers, the agricultural population in many countries is composed of smallholders, tenants, cotters and even métayers, who are not, properly speaking, wage-earners. Furthermore, some smallholders hire out their services at certain periods of the year. On the other hand, agricultural wage-earners sometimes possess land of their own. Further, from the point of view of organisation, agricultural unions and federations are not so clear-cut as those in manufacturing industry. In some countries, like France, there are joint unions of agriculturists which include small farmers and wage-earners. In other countries, co-operative organisations are extremely powerful in the agricultural domain.

In the end, and in order to ensure that all interests should be available for consultation by the Mixed Agricultural Committee, it was decided that in addition to the six members of the Standing Mixed Commission, a panel of experts should be constituted who could be called in to assist as specialists in the consideration of problems of more peculiar interest to them.

The First Session of the Committee was held at Geneva from August 22–24, 1923. The six statutory members were present, together with twelve experts. It was decided, with regard to procedure, that only the statutory members of the Committee should be allowed to vote. The Committee discussed three main questions. The first of these questions was the vocational training of agricultural workers. It will be remembered that a Recommendation of the Third Session of the Conference suggested that each Member of the Organisation should send a report to the Office at regular intervals containing full information as to the administration of vocational agricultural education in their countries. In accordance with this Recommendation, the Office proposed to address to the Governments a detailed questionnaire, and the Committee was consulted with regard to the questions to be inserted in this questionnaire. The experts prepared a draft questionnaire, which was approved by the Committee. The questionnaire covered the following points :—

1. Legislation.
2. Inclusion of agricultural subjects in the curriculum of elementary schools.
3. Continuation classes in agricultural subjects.
4. Special institutions for agricultural education.
5. Agricultural extension education.

The experts considered that on the receipt of the replies to the questionnaire they would be able to compare the legislation in the various countries, the methods adopted and the results achieved, and consequently consider what definite proposals they should present.

One of the Recommendations adopted by the 1921 Session of the Conference, dealing with the prevention of unemployment in agriculture, invited the Governments to examine the possibility of taking steps to encourage the creation of agricultural workers' co-operative societies for the working and purchase, or renting, of land, and of taking steps to this end to increase agricultural credit, especially in favour of co-operative educational associations of land workers established for the purpose of agricultural production, and furthermore, requested the Governments to furnish the Office with periodical reports on the steps taken by them to give effect to these provisions.

The Committee was asked to assist in drawing up a questionnaire to be despatched to the Governments with the object of obtaining from them reports on the questions dealt with in this Recommendation. A questionnaire was duly prepared and approved by the Committee covering the following points :—

1. Co-operative societies for agricultural work.
2. Co-operative societies for the purchase of land.
3. Co-operative societies for the rent of land.
4. Co-operative agricultural credit institutions.

The Committee was invited to express its opinion on the means by which the question of the prevention of anthrax among flocks could be examined. This question was placed on the Agenda of the Committee in accordance with a resolution of the Advisory Committee on Anthrax,[1] to the effect that the International Labour Office should take steps with a view to the further examination of the question of anthrax among flocks, in agreement with the International Institute of Agriculture at Rome. The opinion of the Commission was also asked on certain questions on the Agenda of the Sixth Session of the International Labour Conference, which relate in some measure to agricultural labour.

The decisions of the Commission were submitted to the Governing Body during its Twentieth Session and were unanimously approved.

### III. AD HOC COMMISSIONS.

1. *The Emigration Commission.*—A special Commission to deal with questions of migration met from August 2–11, 1921, in accordance with a resolution of the Washington Conference. The resolution was as follows :—

The Conference resolves that the Governing Body of the International Labour Office shall appoint an International Commission which, while giving due regard to the sovereign rights of each State,

---

[1] The proceedings of this Committee will be mentioned below.

shall consider and report what measures can be adopted to regulate the migration of workers out of their own States and to protect the interests of wage-earners residing in States other than their own, such Commission to present its report at the meeting of the International Labour Conference in 1920.

The representation of European countries on the Commission shall be limited to one-half the total membership of the Commission.

In pursuance of this resolution, the Governing Body appointed a Commission of eighteen members. This Commission is of particular interest from a constitutional standpoint, in view of the extraordinary skill with which a balance was maintained as between Governments, employers and workers, as between European and overseas countries, as between countries of emigration and countries of immigration, and as between large and small Powers. The following list indicates the States represented and the category to which the representatives belong :—

*Government representatives :* Brazil, Canada, China, France, India, Japan.

*Employers' representatives :* Argentine, Czechoslovakia, Greece, South Africa, Spain, Switzerland.

*Workers' representatives :* Australia, Germany, Italy, Poland, Sweden, the United States.

Thus, nine European and nine overseas countries were represented. Seven of these were countries of emigration, seven of immigration and four were countries where the interests of both groups were approximately equal. The representation of countries of trans-Oceanic and Continental emigration was also roughly equal. The Chairman of the Commission was Viscount Ullswater, former Speaker of the British House of Commons.

This Commission was, like all the Commissions of the Office, a purely consultative body. Elaborate preparation had been made for the work of the Commission, and in order to provide it with the necessary information, the International Labour Office drew up a detailed questionnaire consisting of the following three sections :

1. Statistical information and the situation in various countries.
2. Legislation and treaties dealing with migration.
3. The programme of work for the Commission.

This questionnaire was sent to the Governments of all the States Members of the International Labour Organisation. Thirty-two replies were received on the basis of which the Office drew up ten special reports to assist the Commission in the formulation of its decisions. The first eight of these reports related to the following subjects :—

1. Supervision of emigration agents and supply of information to emigrants.
2. Collective recruiting in foreign countries.
3. Deduction from the wages of emigrants of sums advanced before departure.
4. Examination of emigrants before embarkation.
5. Health of emigrants on board ship and on the railways.
6. Insurance of emigrants during the voyage.
7. Finding of employment for emigrants.
8. Equality of treatment of emigrant workers and national workers.

The two main questions submitted to the Emigration Commission by the Washington Conference were :—

1. The regulation of the migration of workers leaving their native country ; and
2. The protection of the interests of workers domiciled in a country other than their country of origin.

On the second point the Commission did not enter into the details of the extremely complicated questions involved. It contented itself with expressing the hope that the largest possible measure of equality of treatment would obtain between nationals and foreigners. As a preliminary, with a view to securing this end, it requested the International Labour Office to prepare reports on an international co-ordination of laws and uniform insurance legislation with a view to the taking of decisions at future Conferences.

In accordance with this decision, the International Labour Office has prepared reports on the subject, and the Governing Body decided to include as one of the items on the Agenda of the 1924 Conference the question of the " Equality of treatment for national and foreign workers as regards Workmen's Compensation for accidents."

With regard to the regulation of migration, the Commission formulated a corpus of twenty-nine resolutions. In each case the resolution aims at remedying some abuse which is particularly prevalent in connection with emigration. In order to realise the scope of the work of the Commission, it will be convenient to set out in order these abuses, together with the remedies which the Commission suggested :—

I. *Abuse.* The intending emigrant is deceived and exploited by emigration agents.

*Remedy.* The Commission proposed the institution of State supervision of the activities of emigration, transport, and recruiting agents, sub-agents, etc. (Resolution X).

II. *Abuse.* Other agents induce him to emigrate under unfavourable conditions.

*Remedy.* Fraudulent inducements to emigrate should be dealt with by repressive measures on the part of the Governments (Resolution XII).

III. *Abuse.* He has no effective redress against insolvent agents who have defrauded him.

*Remedy.* In order to ensure that the emigrant is compensated for any injury he may receive, transport companies should be made jointly responsible for the acts and engagements of their agents and all persons acting in their name or on their account (Resolution XIII).

IV. *Abuse.* In the absence of complete and reliable information he is obliged to have recourse to clandestine agents.

*Remedy.* All available information should be supplied to emigrants by the Governments themselves (Resolution XI). In order to facilitate the supply of information all Governments should immediately forward all available information concerning emigration and immigration to the International Labour Office (Resolution I).

V. *Abuse.* If he applies to collective recruiting agents, he has no guarantee of the conditions under which he will work in the foreign country. Many promises are made to him, but few of them are kept.

*Remedy.* Collective recruiting of labour for foreign countries should only be carried out under the supervision of the authorities by authorised agents or employment agencies, after consultation with employers' and workers' organisations. Suitable wage and labour conditions should be provided, and the contracts should, if possible, be written, and should take account of the state of the labour market in the countries concerned. Collective recruiting should be prohibited in the case of strikes and lock-outs (Resolutions XIV and XV).

VI. *Abuse.* During the journey he suffers from diversity and lack of co-ordination in the legislation of various countries with which he cannot be acquainted. Sometimes sudden changes in legislation interfere with plans which have already been partially carried out.

*Remedy.* The International Labour Office is instructed to study the question of co-ordinating emigration and immigration legislation (Resolution III). It is desirable that, in executing legislation which profoundly modifies that already in force, care should be taken that immigrants do not suffer through precipitate application (Resolution XXVII).

VII. *Abuse.* Bad sanitary conditions often prevail on the railways and on board ship.

*Remedy.* The Commission considered that it would be premature to ask the Governments to set up universal legislation concerning sanitary conditions of emigrants on board ship and on the railways at the present time. In order to prepare for future legislative action, however, it requested the Governing Body to appoint a commission of technical experts to assist the International Labour Office in preparing a report for submission to the International Labour Conference dealing with the minimum conditions of hygiene, safety and comfort to be provided for emigrants on board ship and on the railways (Resolution XXII).

VIII. *Abuse.* Neither the emigrant nor his family have any redress if he is injured in an accident during the journey.

*Remedy.* The Commission proposed that emigrants should be insured against death or disablement en route, from the beginning of the journey until arrival at their destination (Resolution XXIII).

IX. *Abuse.* When the emigrant arrives at his destination after a long and difficult journey, when he has realised his property and broken up his home, he is liable to be refused admission by the country to which he has emigrated.

*Remedy.* In order to prevent the immigrant being refused admission on arrival, the Commission recommended that Governments should arrange for the thorough inspection of emigrants at ports of embarkation and the principal places of transit (Resolution XX). It suggested that special Conventions should be made between the States concerned to settle the conditions under which inspection can take place before embarkation, so that emigrants may be sure of admission to the country of immigration (Resolution XXI).

X. *Abuse.* There is no institution for the protection of the emigrant against the numerous difficulties which confront him when he first lands.

*Remedy.* The Commission proposed that suitable arrangements for the reception and protection of newly arrived immigrants should be organised (Resolution XXVI). With a view to providing adequate protection, it further proposed the investigation of the possibility of providing a common organisation, by agreements between the countries concerned, for the assistance and protection of emigrants of all nationalities at the port of disembarkation or frontier station (Resolution XXIXc).

XI. *Abuse.* His lack of knowledge of the country makes it difficult for him to find suitable employment.

*Remedy.* In order to assist immigrants to find employment, the Commission proposed that each Government should make its national system of employment agencies available for them ; that the employment exchange and emigration organisations should keep in close touch with one another ; that the exchange of information concerning the state of foreign labour markets between the employment agencies of adjoining countries should be facilitated ; and that special employment agencies for emigrants should be set up in places where large numbers of emigrants congregate (Resolutions IV, V, VI and VII).

XII. *Abuse.* Contracts made before emigration, involving deductions from wages or other forms of subjection which are contrary to the customs of the country of immigration, frequently restrict his freedom of movement and the disposal of his labour and his property.

*Remedy.* The Commission proposed that all contracts involving deductions from wages for advances made to emigrants before their departure should be declared null and void if they were contrary to the legislation, regulations or customs of the country of immigration (Resolution XIV).

XIII. *Abuse.* The immigrant is frequently not entitled to the full benefit of laws for the protection of workers. In particular, the application of legislation on insurance benefit and education is often insufficient or defective. Equality of treatment with native workers is not granted.

*Remedy.* The Commission expressed the desire that the largest possible measure of equality of treatment between national and foreign workers should be provided by international Conventions or by legislation, especially as regards labour legislation, social insurance, State relief and the right of association for trade union purposes (Resolution VIII). Children of foreigners should be allowed access to institutions for general and technical education (Resolution XXV).

XIV. *Abuse.* The foreign worker is sometimes subject to arbitrary taxation.

*Remedy.* The Commission proposed that the possibility of the payment by the employer of special taxes falling exclusively upon foreign workers should be investigated (Resolution XXIXA).

XV. *Abuse.* If he contracts an industrial disease in the country of immigration, his labour power, which is his sole source of wealth, may be destroyed without any kind of compensation.

*Remedy.* The Commission proposed the investigation of the question of compensation for emigrants who have contracted an incurable disease after a certain period of work in the territory of the country of immigration, if they had been subject on arrival to an inspection which showed that they were then in a good state of health (Resolution XXIXB).

XVI.  *Abuse.*  These abuses press most hardly on women and children.

*Remedy.* At the request of the special Conference on Traffic in Women and Children, the Commission decided that the protection of emigrants should be applied in particular to women and children, and recognised that the measures which it proposed were calculated to remedy some of the abuses of the traffic in question (Resolutions XVII and XVIII). It is also decided to draw the special attention of the Governments to the question, and proposed that the protection of women and children proceeding from one country to another should be placed on the Agenda of the 1922 Conference (Resolution XIX).

XVII.  *Abuse.*  Certain races are subjected to specially unfavourable treatment.

*Remedy.* After discussing a proposal brought forward by the Chinese delegate, the Commission proposed that the International Labour Conference should place upon its agenda the question of the equality of treatment, from an economic standpoint, and without distinction of country of origin, of all emigrants legally admitted into the country of immigration (Resolution XXVIII).

These resolutions were submitted for consideration to the Governing Body of the Office, which decided that it would be necessary to proceed by stages with a view to international legislation. As a first stage, it placed on the Agenda of the 1922 Conference the question of the communication to the International Labour Office of statistical and other information regarding emigration and immigration and the repatriation and transit of emigrants. It was felt by the Governing Body that the first condition of a fruitful examination of the resolutions of the Emigration Commission with a view to legislation was the centralisation of all statistical and other information regarding migration problems. An account of the discussions and decisions of the 1922 Conference on this matter has already been given.

The Emigration Commission did not, however, confine

itself merely to the adoption of this large body of resolutions. It resolved that the Governing Body of the Office should consider the creation of a permanent Commission to assist the Office in its work, and to follow from day to day, with full moral authority, the development of questions of migration.

It is of interest to note also that a proposal was made to the Commission, but not adopted, to set up a permanent Commission with wide executive powers. The Brazilian delegate, in the name of his Government, proposed the permanent constitution of an International Emigration Commission with a view to directing the migratory current in a reasonable manner from countries where work is scarce to countries where labour is required. This Commission would also be authorised to act as an organ of conciliation in conflicts which might arise between Governments relating to emigration. While sympathy was expressed with this bold idea, the Commission agreed with the views expressed by the Director of the Office, who pointed out the practical difficulties and indeed the dangers, of undertaking risks of ill-defined scope which might be regarded as an infringement of the sovereign rights of States. The Commission, therefore, reluctant to accept a mission of so novel and so delicate a character, confined itself to proposing, as we have seen, that a Permanent Commission should be appointed possessing functions of an advisory character only.

2. *The Advisory Committee on Anthrax.*—The Advisory Committee on Anthrax was set up in accordance with a decision of the Governing Body in January 1922, and in execution of a resolution of the Third Session of the Conference. The terms of reference of the Committee as settled by the Governing Body on the basis of the resolution of the Third Session of the General Conference were as follows :—

The Advisory Committee should be charged with enquiring into—

(a) The problem of the disinfection of wool and hair infected with anthrax spores in all its bearings and to report thereon to the Governing Body in time for consideration by the 1923 Conference ;

(b) The practice and effective methods of preventing infection among flocks, and to report thereon to the 1923 Conference ;

(c) The possibilities of dealing with infection by anthrax from hides and skins and other materials.

Invitations to appoint an expert to take part in the work of the Committee had been addressed to the Governments of the twelve chief wool-producing and manufacturing countries designated by the Governing Body : Australia, Belgium, France, Germany, Great Britain, India, Italy, Japan, Spain, South Africa, Sweden and the United States of America. These invitations were accepted by all the Governments concerned, including the Government of the United States of America, which appointed an expert of the Department of Agriculture to co-operate in an unofficial and advisory capacity with the Committee.

The Committee held ten sittings from December 5–14, 1922. The Committee first dealt with the question of the disinfection of wool and hair infected with anthrax spores and adopted the following resolution :—

The Committee proposes that the Governing Body of the International Labour Office should include on the Agenda of the next Conference a Draft Convention established on the following bases :

1. That hair used in the brush-making and upholstering industry shall be disinfected before the materials are handled industrially ;

2. That wool and hair to be used in the textile industry shall be disinfected before the materials are handled industrially, except in the following cases :

(a) If the country of origin is included in the schedule of areas where the danger is slight ;

(b) If the material imported has already been disinfected by a process recognised as effective ;

(c) In such other cases as may be determined by the authorities mentioned below.

The above-mentioned schedule shall be kept up-to-date each year by the Advisory Committee on Hygiene constituted by the International Labour Office.

Similarly, industrial processes of disinfection shall be approved by the Governing Body of the International Labour Office on the advice of the above Committee, or, if necessary, on the recommendation of the Health Committee of the League of Nations.

At subsequent sittings the Committee considered details of application affecting the above resolution, and the following resolutions corollary to the above resolution were unanimously adopted :—

The Committee is of opinion that paragraph 2 of the resolution should not apply to materials grown in any given country and intended to be used in that country.

Wool and long hair to be used in the textile industry which must be sorted before washing shall not be required to be disinfected except in the case of such classes of these materials as may be excluded from the schedule of non-dangerous materials referred to under 2 of the resolution.

The Committee also examined the question of the prevention of infection by anthrax from hides and skins, and recommended that regulations be laid down in the different countries, having for their object the protection of the workers and the soil against infection from anthrax from hides and skins.

Dealing with the question of the prevention of anthrax infection among flocks, the Committee agreed that this question was primarily within the competence of the International Institute of Agriculture at Rome.

The Committee also examined measures for the protection of workers handling animal products, such as bones, horns and hoofs, and expressed the opinion that horns and hoofs should be sterilised before being subjected to any industrial operation.

The report of this Committee was presented to the Governing Body at its Session of April 1923, which decided to submit it to a subsequent Conference for decision on the action which it appeared desirable to take.

### IV. COMMITTEES OF EXPERTS.

The general character of the Committees of Experts appointed by the Office has already been indicated. It will be enough, therefore, to mention the Committees which have already been appointed and to give a brief outline of their work.

From the constitutional point of view, these Committees present little interest. Their importance resides in the valuable work which they can accomplish as Committees of Experts on obscure and difficult questions in advising the Office on steps which it is necessary and practicable to take.

1. *Advisory Committee on Industrial Hygiene.*—It has already been mentioned that the importance of industrial hygiene was fully recognised by the First Session of the International Labour Conference. That Conference was not content to adopt once and for all Draft Conventions and Recommendations. It considered that it was imperative also that the permanent organ of the Organisation, the Office, should be in a position to deal with all questions relating to industrial hygiene with the necessary authority. The Commission on Unhealthy Processes of the Conference, in its report, proposed that " a Health Section should be formed in the International Labour Office which would keep in touch with the Medical Departments of the Government Offices charged with the application of Factory Laws." The Conference itself, on the proposal of Dr. Miall, technical adviser to the British employers' delegate, adopted the following resolution :—

That an Advisory Committee, on which the Governments, the employers and the workers should all be represented, be appointed to act in an auxiliary capacity and to keep in touch with the activities of the Health Department of the International Labour Office.

In pursuance of this resolution, an Advisory Committee on Industrial Hygiene has been duly constituted and has commenced to work. The Governing Body had some difficulty in reaching a decision as to its composition. At its meeting on April 12, 1921, the Governing Body decided on the creation of a Commission, to be regarded principally as a Correspondence Commission, composed of a fairly large number of members from each country with whom the Office and its Technical Service of Industrial Health would keep in close contact by means of correspondence. The Governing Body again, however, discussed the question during its Ninth Session, and was of the opinion that it might be useful to have alongside the technical experts on the question the direct representation of organised employers and workers. The Commission, as constituted on the original plan, met at the Office on October 22, 1921, and was consulted as to the form which its constitution should take. It was the unanimous opinion that it should be a purely scientific committee. In January 1922 the Governing Body re-considered the question, and decided that the Advisory Committee on Industrial Hygiene should be exclusively technical in character, no attempt being made to give representation to various interests.

It was agreed that collaboration between the experts, the number of whom was not limited, and the Office should be carried out essentially by correspondence, and that a small number of meetings attended by experts particularly competent in the questions to be examined might be held whenever a direct exchange of views might seem desirable. In order to ensure liaison between the Health Committee of the League of Nations and the Advisory Committee on Industrial Hygiene of the International Labour Office, it was decided that the Health Committee of the League should be invited to have a representative on the Committee. In accordance with the decisions arrived at, the International Labour Office communicated with experts of undoubted authority and of different nationalities and requested them to serve on the Committee.

The first meeting of experts was held from September 13–15, 1923, and was attended by nine experts of international standing on industrial health. The Committee considered in the first place the information concerning unhealthy occupations already collected by the Industrial Health Service of the International Labour Office, and unanimously approved the plan of work adopted. It was decided that the publication, in which this information should be issued, should be entitled " Occupation and Health." The attention of the Office had been specially drawn by the Washington Conference to the desirability of compiling a list of unhealthy processes. The report of the Commission on Unhealthy Processes expressly stated, " It should be referred to the International Labour Office to draw up a list of the principal processes to be considered as unhealthy." In accordance with this, the Industrial Health Section has been engaged on the preparation of this list. For each unhealthy process a special article is being compiled containing a statement of the technical organisation of the industry or process and of the special dangers which it involves. Information will also be given on industrial pathology, special health measures and legislation regarding each process or industry classified as unhealthy or dangerous.

With a view to ensuring that each subject shall be treated from an international point of view, the Office has taken steps to obtain the collaboration not only of members of the Advisory Committee on Industrial Hygiene, but also of the most eminent experts of various countries. More than thirty scientists have so far assured the Office of their assistance in the preparation of about one hundred articles dealing with the most important industrial poisons and unhealthy processes.

The Advisory Committee on Industrial Hygiene also discussed the organisation of research concerning the disinfection of hides and skins infected with anthrax spores. The Committee formulated in detail a certain number of recommendations on the method of organisation and the scope of the research work to be carried out, and also on the problem of the disinfection of effluents of tanneries and of the early application of anti-anthrax serum.

The question of the disinfection of hides and skins infected with anthrax spores had been referred to the Committee by the Advisory Committee on Anthrax.

2. *Conference of Experts on Disablement.*—The Governing Body, at its Session of October 1921, authorised the Director to convene a Conference consisting of experts in matters relating to men disabled in the War. At the Session held in January 1922, the Governing Body further approved the constitution of a Conference of Experts consisting of six experts nominated

by agreement with the most important associations for the disabled in France, Great Britain, Italy, Germany, Austria and Poland, four experts from Government Departments dealing with this question in France, Great Britain, Italy and Germany, and one representative each from the Health Section of the League of Nations, the League of Red Cross Societies, the International Red Cross Committee and the Permanent Inter-Allied Committee of the Disabled.

The Governing Body of the Office was led to take such action as a consequence of the desires which had been formulated by the various large associations of disabled men in the chief belligerent countries for information with regard to divers aspects of the problem which interested them. The problems on which the associations approached the International Labour Office for information were various. The English disabled suffered from the unemployment crisis, and asked to be informed on the organisation of the employment of war disabled in other countries. The French disabled were more particularly concerned with their Pensions Law, and were anxious to obtain information with regard to what had been done in other countries. The Italian disabled asked for information on the compulsory employment of the disabled in Germany and in Austria, and, above all, for particulars with regard to emigration. The German disabled were concerned with the rational distribution of the labour of the disabled on the labour market.

It became clear both to Governments and to the associations of disabled men that it was necessary that an international investigation should be conducted into all questions relating to disabled workers. As early as 1920, the British Government had suggested that this investigation should be entrusted to the International Labour Office and the International Health Organisation. A meeting of delegates of the federations of ex-Service men of France, Great Britain, Italy, Germany, Austria and Poland, which met at Geneva on September 12, 1921, drew up a programme of demands relating to the conditions of work, to prosthesis, to social insurance and to the international protection of the disabled, which they addressed to the Office. It was in consequence, therefore, of this need which had been spontaneously expressed both by the associations of ex-Service men and by Governments that the International Labour Office called this Conference.

The following Agenda was considered at the Conference :—

1. Proposed organisation of an international exhibition of artificial limbs and orthopædic instruments.
2. Comparative study of the administrative organisation of prosthesis and orthopædic treatment.
3. Comparative study of the administrative organisation of medical aid for war disabled.

The Conference was attended by nine experts. They reached the following general conclusions, which apply equally to the three questions figuring on the Agenda :—

(a) The great progress accomplished in each country as regards prosthesis, orthopædic treatment and medical aid is not sufficiently known in other countries, and it is urgently necessary in the immediate interest of war disabled and in the permanent interest of the victims of industrial accidents that full and accurate information on these subjects should be generally diffused.

(b) Legislation concerning industrial accidents should be amended in such a way as to allow men disabled in industry to receive artificial limbs and orthopædic and medical treatment for an unlimited period.

(c) It is necessary and urgent that disabled men living in countries other than their own should be provided with artificial limbs and orthopædic and medical treatment.

Detailed resolutions were adopted on each of the questions on the Agenda. They refer in the first place to the laying-down of certain general principles for the administrative organisation of prosthesis and the administrative organisation of medical assistance. The experts further requested the International Labour Organisation to take the initiative in the organisation of a centre for the collection of information and an institution for research and for scientific publications, and to organise an exhibition of artificial limbs and orthopædic instruments. Finally, for the protection of disabled persons residing outside of their own country, the experts laid down the general principles according to which agreements might be drawn up between States in order to ensure to their disabled the benefits of medical assistance and prosthesis. They requested the Office to communicate their conclusions on this point to all Governments, and supply Governments with any information which might facilitate the conclusion of agreements, and to do everything in its power to ensure that in any agreements concluded regard might be had for the principle unanimously agreed upon by the experts as the most desirable.

The resolutions adopted were duly submitted to the Governing Body. During the course of its Twelfth and Thirteenth Sessions, in April and July 1922, the Governing Body examined them, and decided that the Director should communicate to the Governments concerned the conclusions of the experts with regard to the international protection of the disabled, and that the Director should place himself at the disposal of the Governments to furnish them with all information likely to facilitate the conclusions of agreements. With regard to prosthesis, the Governing Body considered that it was not expedient to organise an international exhibition, but it decided on the preparation of a book concerning vocational re-education and containing photographs of appliances, sketches and explanatory notes illustrating the progress accomplished since the War.

Steps have already been taken to give effect to these resolutions of the experts.

The Minister for Social Welfare of the Czechoslovak Republic, on being informed of the resolution adopted by the experts, requested the International Labour Office to lend its assistance in the conclusion of a reciprocal agreement between the Czechoslovak Republic and Germany. The International Labour Office has forwarded to the German Government the request of the Czechoslovak Ministry, and has indicated that the Office is ready to lend its assistance to the two Governments if they are both of the opinion that agreement may be reached.

A further meeting of experts for the purpose of investigating the problem of finding employment for disabled men opened at Geneva on July 31, 1923. Experts representing thirteen countries took part in this meeting. Recent statistics have shown that the total number of war disabled is at least ten millions, including eight millions who, in spite of their pensions, are forced to a varying extent to look for work. Placed by their disablement in a position of inferiority on the labour market, they often find preference given to able-bodied workers. Owing to the difficulty of determining their degree of technical ability, serious difficulties often arise in fixing their wages. In periods of unemployment, moreover, disabled workers suffer more directly and seriously than others.

The object of the meeting of experts at Geneva was to examine the general problem of placing disabled men, after an exchange of information on the solutions effected or adopted in different countries, the difficulties met with and the results obtained.

The experts found themselves in agreement on the importance of the problem of finding employment for the disabled, and the urgent need for a solution in the interests both of the disabled, whose sacrifices entitle them to a secure and adequate subsistence, and of the different national communities, which, by rationally organising disabled labour, will secure that the disabled are in a position to do all the work of which they are capable, and that all the forces of production are utilised.

The conclusions of the experts were formulated first in certain " fundamental principles," and secondly in certain " essential provisions " intended to be included in all legislation, regulations, or agreements, relating to finding employment for disabled men.

The experts expressed their unanimous opinion that special measures of protection for securing the employment of the disabled should apply to all disabled persons who, owing to some infirmity, have acquired the right to a pension. They maintained that disabled labour should be distributed among all undertakings with the exception of those employing less than a certain minimum number of persons. They also considered that in calculating the staff both men and women workers should be taken into account.

The experts then considered the question of the exemptions which might be granted in the interests either of the disabled themselves or of the undertaking by the bodies which administer the law, after consulting the industrial organisations concerned and associations of the disabled. They expressed the view that undertakings profiting from such exemptions should be under the obligation to pay a tax, the revenue from which would be paid into a central fund to be used on behalf of unemployed disabled.

The experts considered that legislation or schemes for voluntary collaboration intended to secure employment for all the disabled should fix a general percentage applicable to all undertakings, account being taken of the number of able-bodied wage-earners in each country. Exemptions from the general percentage could be granted to certain groups of undertakings in which the employment of the disabled is particularly difficult. Such exemptions would be granted by bodies in which the industrial associations concerned and the associations of the disabled would be represented.

3. *Committee of Experts on Social Insurance.*—The attention of the Governing Body during its Eighth Session was called by the Director to the fact that the old Permanent Committee for Social Insurance had not functioned since the War, and that it would be of use to the Office if international co-operation in this matter could be re-established. The Director was empowered by the Governing Body to invite experts of recognised competence in the matter of social insurance to meet at Geneva in order to study the question of the establishment of a Committee of Correspondence to co-ordinate work with regard to social insurance in various countries.

Six experts met at Geneva on September 22, 1921,

and expressed the view that the institution of a Correspondence Committee would be of great value to the Office. A few days afterwards, on November 4, 1921, an unofficial meeting was held at Geneva, attended by a certain number of delegates and advisers to the Third Session of the Conference specially interested in questions of Social Insurance. This meeting also declared itself in favour of the institution of a body to assist the Office in its work in connection with this subject. In accordance with the views thus expressed, the Office has constituted a Correspondence Committee, consisting of fifteen experts drawn from various countries.

As this Committee is primarily a Correspondence Committee, it has never been called upon to meet, but important correspondence has been conducted with it.

4. *Correspondence Committee on Co-operation.*—A Correspondence Committee of technical experts in matters relating to the various aspects of the co-operative movement has also been constituted. This action was taken in pursuance of the spirit of a resolution of the Fourth Session of the International Labour Conference. In adopting this resolution, the Conference considered that co-operative organisations, through their increasingly numerous undertakings in commerce, industry and agriculture, both in European and non-European countries, form a factor in the economic life of the world which cannot be neglected, and that, in consequence, it should be possible for them to be able to give their opinion directly on questions of labour legislation affecting them to the same degree as private enterprises.

The Committee which has been established consists of persons recommended by the best qualified co-operative organisations of various tendencies in the different countries. This Correspondence Committee brings experts in different forms of co-operation into close touch with each other and with the Office, and is contributing already to give the principles and practical realisation of co-operation a more important place than heretofore in the work of the International Labour Office.

This Committee has already been asked for its opinion

with regard to the problem of night work in baking, a question concerning intimately the work of the large co-operative societies, which appears on the Agenda of the 1924 Session of the Conference.

It will be realised from the above enumeration that International Commissions have played, and continue to play, an extremely important part in the general work of the International Labour Organisation. The criticism has, indeed, been made that there are too many Commissions, and further, that the multiplication of such Commissions might tend to prevent the Office itself from exercising initiative. It is, however, easy to reply to these criticisms. In the first place, the Commissions which have been set up have in all cases been established to respond to a real need which has been widely felt. In most cases, they have been established in direct pursuance of a resolution of the Conference itself, and in order to secure expert assistance to the Office in the preparation for the work of the Conference of information on questions on which the adoption of international Conventions or Recommendations would appear to be desirable. Without the assistance of such Commissions of specialists, it would be impossible for the Office to prepare the necessary information with the moral authority which can only come from technical knowledge and experience. The second criticism will be seen to be of little importance if attention is paid to the variety and elasticity of the Commissions which have been established. In some cases, as has been indicated, the Commissions are of a formal and strictly official character. In other cases, they are of a semi-official nature. Particular kinds of Commissions have been established in order to meet the needs that have been felt in particular circumstances, and it would be true to say that in many cases the initiative of the Office itself has been fostered, and not restricted, by the existence of Committees, various in their constitution and in the subjects with which they deal, but united in their desire to assist in the establishment of humane conditions by means of international labour legislation throughout the world.

# CHAPTER IX

## INTERNATIONAL INFORMATION

It was intended by the framers of Part XIII of the Treaty that the International Labour Office should become not only an international bureau of research but also an international clearing house of information on all questions relating to labour and industry.

One of the two main functions expressly assigned to the International Labour Office by the Treaty of Peace is " the collection and distribution of information on all subjects relating to the international adjustment of conditions of industrial life and labour, and particularly the examination of subjects which it is proposed to bring before the Conference with a view to the conclusion of international conventions, and the conduct of such special investigations as may be ordered by the Conference."

The collection and distribution of information is therefore an important part of the work of the Office. It will be convenient to consider first the collection and detailed treatment of information, and later its distribution. It is clear that collection naturally comes before distribution. It is impossible, except for the " bear " on the Stock Exchange, to distribute what has not been previously collected. The Office was, however, called upon in its early days to try to perform this impossible task.

As early as 1920, immediately after the Organisation came into being, large numbers of requests for information began to pour into the Office. This was an encouraging sign of the need that was widely experienced of such an organisation, but the satisfaction which was felt at this obvious indication that the Office had a real function to perform, was tempered by the difficulties which were immediately experienced in supplying the information required. The Office had been in existence only a week or two ; it had no archives ; it had no library. The members of the staff were just beginning to arrive ; difficulties of language, which have now to a very considerable extent been overcome, were enormous.

Information was asked for on such subjects as the extent to which collective agreements had been made in various countries to provide for the variation of wages in accordance with the cost of living. The Office was asked to state the number of coal miners in various countries who were organised in craft unions or in industrial unions. Now the information necessary to reply to questions of this technical kind does not usually exist in books. It is necessary to get the information at first hand from the organisations concerned in the various countries.

Owing to the relations which the Office has now been able to establish with Governments, trade unions, employers' associations, universities, etc., in the various countries, it has collected in its archives a vast quantity of information on such technical subjects in the world of labour and industry, and when requests of a similar kind reach the Office now, it is usually able to satisfy them in a very short time by drawing on the sources of information which have been accumulated. In the early days, however, this was not the case, and it was with the greatest difficulty that the Office succeeded in obtaining the information necessary to send to its correspondents. There can be no doubt, however, that the efforts which the Office put forward, and the goodwill which it showed, in trying to satisfy these earlier requests, have borne fruit in the excellence of the relations which have continued to subsist between it and the organisations concerned, and the frequency with which they now have recourse to the Office to satisfy their requirements.

It is now necessary to go into some detail in explain-

ing the machinery which has been established at the
Office for collecting information.

1. *The Collection of Information.*—The collection of
information is undertaken by a group of departments
in the Office. This group of departments is closely
organised and forms, in spirit at least, one unit, but
the principle of specialisation of function makes it
necessary that the various tasks involved in the collection,
indexing and preservation of information should be distributed among various groups of workers. These groups,
however, work in the closest possible co-operation.

The first of the Services of the Office concerned with
the collection of information is naturally the Library.
One of the earliest duties of the Office has been to
collect as large a number as possible of the publications which may be useful for its investigations. At
the present time the Organisation covers fifty-seven
States ; almost all of these publish a large amount of
official information on labour and industry. Unofficial
publications appearing in the principal industrial countries are still more numerous. These include reports of
trade unions and employers' associations, statistical and
other studies published by various institutes, reports of
national and international conferences, and publications
concerning each of the numerous aspects of the labour
problem.

The basis of the Library of the Office was formed by
the library set up at Basle by the International Association for Labour Legislation. This office possessed
a well-stocked library consisting principally of documents which had been regularly provided by public
administrative bodies. This nucleus has been continually
added to at a very rapid rate. The average weekly
number of fresh books and pamphlets acquired by the
Library has been 700. The average weekly number
of periodicals received is 900. The catalogue of the
Library at present includes about 130,000 different
publications in some thirty languages. The extraordinarily rapid rate at which the Library is increasing
leads to the hope that before many years have elapsed,

it will provide for the purposes of research work the largest and most complete collection in existence of matter relating to industry and labour.

Two special characteristics of the Library should be mentioned. One of the aims of the Library is that it should become a centre to which research students from all countries interested in labour and industrial questions will resort for study. M. Bergson has emphasised the fact that in the case of all scientific work it is indispensable to constitute a number of centres where there is a certainty of finding all the publications on any particular subject. In its own sphere the International Labour Office considers that it ought to attempt to carry out M. Bergson's suggestion and become the international centre with the completest collection of books and pamphlets in its particular field. Although the Library has been in existence for less than four years, it is already becoming known, and research workers from a considerable number of countries have applied for and have been granted opportunities to study in the Library. When the new building, which is at present being erected for the Office, has been completed, special accommodation will be set apart for research workers, and there can be little doubt that the utility of the Office in this connection will rapidly increase.

The most important function of the Library is naturally to act as a circulating agency within the Office. It is not merely a receptacle into which books and periodicals are deposited. It is definitely a workshop library. One of its chief tasks is to ensure that books and periodicals which reach the Office are seen by the Service or Services interested. It is responsible for the regular distribution in the Office of all newspapers and periodicals, and for the preparation and distribution of a fortnightly accession list which draws the attention of the various Services of the Office to new books likely to be of importance to their particular work.

Alongside the Library is a special Service called the Documents Service, which is responsible for keeping a collection of Press cuttings and similar fugitive documents which are indispensable for the work of the Office. It is important to keep such collections of information, not only for the study of current events and tendencies, but also from the point of view of history. The historian of the future who attempts to write the industrial history of his country, will find that it is more and more difficult to do justice to the various trends of thought and feeling which move the masses of the workers without consulting files or cuttings of the daily Press. This Service, in addition, collects and classifies all collective agreements. The importance of collective agreements, particularly in the fixing of hours of labour and wages, is constantly increasing, and it has become particularly necessary that the Office should have on file the collective agreements made in the most important industrial countries. The texts of these agreements form part of the stock-in-trade of the Office. The Office has also proceeded to institute a very interesting collection of the rules and constitutions of trade unions and employers' associations. It is often necessary to know what is the constitution of a trade union or an employers' association if the attitude of such an association in a dispute is to be properly understood.

In addition to the information which reaches the Office more or less automatically in printed form, it is necessary for it frequently to obtain information which is not published. The obvious and natural way in which to obtain information of this kind is to write for it. This the Office naturally does. It has on file exhaustive lists of organisations and individuals who are likely to be able to supply information on various questions for its own publications or for replying to requests for information addressed to it.

In certain cases, however, the information which it is desired to obtain is of such an elaborate type that it is impossible to secure it by means of a simple letter. In these cases the system of the questionnaire is adopted. This method of collecting information on an international scale on the highly technical questions with which the

Office is frequently concerned has proved to be of great value. Such questionnaires must, of course, be drawn up with great care. Great accuracy must be employed in preparing them in order that the questions may be stated in the most explicit possible manner with a view to avoiding the dissipation of energy on the part of the person who replies to them. Further, only the questions which are absolutely essential must be asked in order that the person who replies to the questionnaire may not be overwhelmed with unnecessary detail. The Office has also found that it is essential that questionnaires should be sent out only when it is impossible to obtain the information either in printed documents or by simple letter. Both public administrations and unofficial organisations are overwhelmed with requests for information, and they devote the attention necessary to giving replies to such questionnaires only when they are convinced that the questionnaire is drawn up by persons who really understand the question at issue.

The method of the questionnaire is invariably followed in the preliminary examination of questions which it has been decided to discuss at the meetings of the Conference. To take an example, the Governing Body of the Office has decided that at the 1924 Conference the question of providing for a twenty-four hours' rest per week in glass factories where tank furnaces are used should be considered. This is obviously a highly technical question. In preparing for discussion at the Conference the Office first collects information which it is able to get together from printed documents. This enables it to obtain a general view of the matter, sufficient at any rate to know the right questions to ask in order to secure detailed information. On the basis of this general information which is at its disposal, it prepares a series of questions designed to elicit the further particulars that will be necessary to enable the Conference to discuss the matter fruitfully. This series of questions is then sent to Governments in the various countries with a request for replies. On the basis of the information which is communicated to the Office, it prepares a reasoned and detailed report on the facts of the matter. This report is essential to an enlightened discussion of the question at the Conference.

In other cases questionnaires are sent out in connection with matters not to be discussed at the Conference. An example of this may be given. In November 1920 the Taylor Society of the United States, a society of employment managers and others interested in the scientific organisation of industry, requested the Office to supply it with information on the extent to which the three-shift system had been established in the iron and steel industry in Europe. This information was required, not to satisfy a merely theoretical interest, but in view of the demand which was being made by public opinion in the United States for the adoption of the three-shift system in the iron and steel industry in that country. The Office, on commencing its enquiry, discovered that extremely little had been published on this question, and it realised that in order to be able to supply to the Taylor Society the information desired, it would be necessary to send out questionnaires to the Governments and to the workers' and employers' organisations in the countries in which the iron and steel industry was important. A detailed questionnaire was therefore prepared. It was intended to determine how far the three-shift system had replaced the two-shift system, what effect the application of the three-shift system had had as regards increases in the number of men required to carry it through, the effect upon output, the quality of production, labour costs, the effect of the introduction of the system upon the accident rate, the health of the workers, their efficiency and the use made by them of their leisure.

This questionnaire was translated into five languages and given a wide diffusion. Governments, workers' organisations and employers' organisations of sixteen different countries sent information to the Office, and it was found possible to prepare a lengthy report on the question, which was not only communicated to the

Taylor Society of the United States, but issued in a special publication by the Office.

In a certain number of cases, however, it is impossible for the Office to obtain the necessary information either by consulting public documents or writing letters or by sending out questionnaires. It is necessary that, in addition to the fragmentary information which it obtains in these ways, it should conduct an enquiry on the spot. In such cases, which are not numerous but are usually of special importance, the Office sends an official to the country concerned to enquire on the spot into the state of the question. For instance, when the British Government requested the Office for information with regard to a new system for dealing with unemployment set up at Altona in Germany, the Office instructed one of its officials, who happened at that time to be in Berlin, to go to Altona and collect the necessary information. Similarly in May 1920, when the question of production in the Ruhr Basin had assumed an important place in European relations, an investigator was sent to the spot. In both cases the information obtained has proved extremely valuable. In other cases the enquiries undertaken by the Office have been on a much more elaborate scale, and have involved questions of an important constitutional and political character. Reference to such enquiries will be made later. Mention may, however, be made at this point of an enquiry which has involved all the types of action already mentioned. For this enquiry printed documents were consulted, letters were written, questionnaires were despatched, and officials of the Office conducted enquiries on special points in various countries.

The enquiry into production was undertaken in accordance with a decision taken by the Governing Body on June 9, 1920, on a suggestion made by M. Pirelli, the Italian employers' representative. This enquiry has continued for over three years, and its results are now being published in four volumes. Questionnaires were issued in no fewer than sixteen languages and widely distributed to Governments, workers' and employers' organisations and co-operative associations. An official of the Office made a series of tours of investigation in the following countries : Germany, Kingdom of the Serbs, Croats and Slovenes, Bulgaria, Turkey, Roumania, Poland, Czechoslovakia, Austria, Hungary, Denmark, Sweden and Norway. The enquiry was received in certain quarters with hostility. In certain countries where the question of international competition was the first consideration, anxiety was entertained lest the Office should wittingly or unwittingly serve the special interests of other countries. In spite of opposition the amount of information supplied to the Office has been enormous. No fewer than twenty-nine Governments replied to the questionnaire, and over a thousand workers' and employers' organisations. The work of collating and translating the information has naturally been Herculean.

To assist the Office in its work of collecting and integrating information on particular subjects, various international Commissions have been set up. Detailed reference has already been made to these Commissions and to the results of their work in relation to the action of the International Labour Office. It will be sufficient here, therefore, simply to mention that their work has been of the greatest importance to the Office in connection also with its scientific labours.

2. *Internal Utilisation of Information.*—But who uses all this information within the Office? The information collected is utilised partly by the National Information Section of the Office and partly by the various technical services in the Research Division.

The system of organisation in the National Information Section and in the Research Division differs, and differs for two reasons. In the first place the experience which the Office has acquired has shown that the information which it collects must be utilised for two different purposes on two different levels. It is necessary that the Office should follow carefully current events in the world of labour and industry. It must keep its knowledge up-to-date of what happens in the various countries, and for that purpose it must follow carefully, the daily Press and periodicals, not only in view of the action the Office may be called upon to take in connection with the development and encouragement of International Labour Legislation, but also in order that its publications may contain information that is accurate and up-to-date.

But it is also necessary for the Office to be organised in such a way as to enable it to undertake elaborate enquiries involving extended research. The close following of current events and the undertaking of elaborate research lasting two or three years, as in the case of the enquiry into production, are quite separate tasks which cannot be undertaken by the same persons. Therefore, special services have been set up in the Research Division of the Office to deal with such special subjects as statistics, unemployment, agricultural questions, industrial hygiene, safety and so on.

The second main reason for this differentiation of organisation in the National Information Section on the one hand and the Research Division on the other is due to difficulties of language.

The Office receives a very large amount of information in Government reports and other official documents, periodicals and newspapers, in languages such as Japanese, Polish, Czech, Serbian, Finnish and other languages of an " exotic " character. It is essential that the Office should be able to utilise this information in the interests of the completeness of its scientific research. The National Information Section contains representatives of nineteen different nationalities, and very few written languages are unknown to some or other of the members of this section. These men may be considered to be experts by language, whereas in the Research Division the experts are experts by subject. Now the expert by subject who is a specialist in, say, Industrial Hygiene, is very unlikely to be able to read documents in Japanese, Serbian, Polish, Czech and other languages. If he wishes to utilise these documents he must have recourse to the assistance of the specialist by language. Now the specialist by language is not an expert on industrial hygiene, but by close co-operation between the expert on the language and the expert on the subject, the Office is moderately certain to be able to utilise accurately and with full understanding of the circumstances the information which reaches it on all subjects.

In spite of every endeavour, the language difficulty remains a real one for the Office. It suggested, in fact, to the first chief of the Research Division the following law : " The difficulty of gathering, compiling and publishing information increases with the number of languages involved, not in simple direct ratio, but in the cube of the number of languages involved."

3. *The Distribution of Information.*—From the first the Office has considered that its work would be of little avail if it contented itself simply with collecting information and utilising it for its own needs. Ultimately such collection of information together with all the work of classification and utilisation is justifiable only if the information thus collected can be usefully distributed. Special attention has therefore been given to the distribution of information. Such distribution can be performed in two ways: on the one hand, by replying to particular requests for information from Governments and associations; on the other hand, by issuing publications and giving them a wide circulation.

*Replies to Enquiries.*—Requests for information reach the Office in large numbers from Governments, employers' and workers' organisations, public and private administrations, universities, libraries, philanthropic and other institutions, as well as from individuals, belonging to most of the States Members of the Organisation. The Office has from the first tried to satisfy these requests in the fullest possible degree, but it has naturally always taken into account the importance of the institution making the request. Thus, it has always considered it its duty to make very special efforts to respond adequately to the applications of Governments, and it has always done its best to reply to requests for information addressed to it by organisations of workers and employers, as these are officially represented in the Organisation. In reply to other classes of requests for information, it finds that it is more and more able to supply the information requested in the form of back numbers of its various publications.

When Governments request information, they frequently state that the particulars are required with a view to the preparation of new national laws or administrative measures. In such cases, the Office enables Governments to avoid the expense that would be necessitated by the undertaking of special research, and contributes directly to the development of industrial and labour legislation.

A considerable proportion of the requests for information that are received from Governments come from the States established since the signing of the Treaty of Peace which, in endeavouring to set up a system of labour and industrial legislation, find the expert assistance which the Office is able to render to them of the greatest value. It would be tedious to give a detailed list of the information supplied by the Office in response to these particular requests, but two or three examples of a typical kind may be mentioned.

As examples of requests made by new States for information directly necessary to them in connection with their labour legislation, reference may be made to information supplied to the Government of Esthonia with regard to legislation and regulations dealing with the period of apprenticeship, examination of apprentices and wages of apprentices. The Office was able to supply information with regard to the position in Austria, Bulgaria, Denmark, Germany, Japan, Roumania, Russia, Serbia, South Australia and the United States. In response to a request from the Polish Government, the Office supplied detailed information with regard to days regarded as public holidays in Germany, the Argentine, Belgium, Great Britain, Japan, Switzerland and Czechoslovakia, and also with regard to the practice in various countries according to which a period of vacation with pay is granted to manual and non-manual workers. On both of these questions legislation was envisaged by the Polish Government.

But it is not only the newly established States that find it useful to obtain information from the Office. Large number of requests are received from the Governments of France, Great Britain, Italy, Germany and other States. For example, the Office has supplied information to the Ministry of Industry and Commerce in Paris on the organisation of Government inspection in the merchant marine of the principal countries of the world. It has given information to the Ministry of Labour in Rome on the arrangements in a number of countries for the representation of trade unions on commissions and other advisory bodies set up by the Government to deal with labour and industrial questions. To the Norwegian Department for Social Affairs it has supplied information with regard to the provisions regulating arbitration and conciliation in various countries, and to the Swiss Federal Labour Office it sent detailed information with regard to the rates of unemployment benefit paid in Germany, Australia, Austria, Belgium, Chile, Denmark, Spain, Finland, France, Great Britain, Italy, Luxembourg, the Netherlands, Sweden and Czechoslovakia. To the German Ministry of Labour the Office was able to send an interesting collection of information dealing with the measures taken in various countries to provide for continuation school education for persons employed in the mining industry.

Mention might be made also of the information sent for the use of the United States Coal Commission at the special request of Mr. Secretary Hoover. This information included particulars concerning output, prices, wages, hours of labour, organisation in the industry of both employers and workers, terms of the principal mining laws, provisions of labour laws as regards hygiene and safety, employment of women and children, settlement of industrial disputes, accident statistics and compensation, social insurance and

13

housing, in such countries as Great Britain, France, Belgium and Germany. Some material was also supplied, principally as to output, hours of work, organisation and labour legislation in the coal-mining industry in Czechoslovakia. For Poland, data as to output and wages were furnished.

To British Government Departments also the Office has been able to supply useful information with regard to the training of unemployed workpeople and other subjects.

The Dominions and India have also found the Office of use. The South African Government, when it was examining the question of making provision for unemployment insurance, obtained through the Office a complete collection of all legislation existing in the world on this subject. The Department of Labour in New Zealand, where the question of providing supplementary wages for married men in accordance with the size of their families has for some time been under consideration, has applied to the Office and received information with regard to the measures that have already been taken in providing family wages, varying in accordance with the number of children, in France, Germany and Czechoslovakia. The newly established Bombay Labour Office has frequently turned to the Office for information on various subjects, from the methods of providing conciliation and arbitration machinery in case of labour disputes, down to the qualities desirable in the local correspondents of a Labour Office.

In practically all the cases that have been mentioned so far, the information has been desired by Governments with a view to the drafting of legislation or the making of administrative decrees or orders.

Owing to the extent to which the International Labour Office has developed as an " international clearing-house of industrial and labour information," many Governments have been able to realise direct economies in their administration. When, for example, the German Ministry of Labour was recently reorganised, no special Intelligence Section was set up, as it was considered that each of the administrative services concerned would be able to obtain the information that they required with regard to the practice in foreign countries from the International Labour Office. In Norway and Sweden, which had appointed social attachés to reside in the capitals of the most important industrial countries in order to keep their own Governments informed with regard to labour and industrial progress, the number of such social attachés has already been cut down on the ground that the International Labour Office centralises the information which the social attachés were appointed to collect, and therefore renders unnecessary the maintenance of social attachés in the various capitals.

## THE PUBLICATIONS OF THE OFFICE.

The list of publications issued by the Office during its short existence is already imposing. It has, indeed, been reproached with publishing too much. Each of its publications, however, has a definite purpose. The following are the most important publications of the Office.

*Official Bulletin.*—The Office publishes an official Bulletin. This contains the official records of the Office, a summary of the reports of meetings of the Governing Body, correspondence with Governments of public interest, and official information concerning the ratification of Conventions.

*Industrial and Labour Information.*—A publication of a lighter character is the *Industrial and Labour Information*. This appears once a week and contains information of current interest relating to events and tendencies in the world of labour and industry. This publication originally appeared daily in the interest of giving information with as little delay as possible, but after eighteen months it was decided that as its circulation is largely in distant countries, daily publication was not essential. It now, therefore, appears weekly. The information is presented in a form designed to enable the reader to obtain a quick survey of the most important events relating to labour and industry in the various countries. Information is obtained, not only from official reports and from the Press, but also from the correspondence of the Office, and from telegraphic and other despatches from Governments.

*The International Labour Review.*—This publication, which appears monthly, contains, in addition to special signed articles by experts, monthly surveys on each of the questions with which the Office deals. As far as possible these surveys do not content themselves with giving in juxtaposition facts with regard to the development in the various countries of the question under consideration, but attempt to draw international comparisons and reach conclusions of international interest. It is now felt that there is a real place for an International Review which attempts to compare the results realised and the endeavours made in the various countries in the field of international labour legislation.

*Studies and Reports.*—In addition to these three publications, the Office issues from time to time important special studies or reports in a series entitled " Studies and Reports." In this series are issued the results of important enquiries and investigations conducted by the Office, such as Remedies for Unemployment ; Wage Changes in Various Countries, 1914–1922 ; the Organisation of Industry and Labour Conditions in Soviet Russia ; the Protection of Eyesight in Industry ; the Problems and Methods of Vocational Guidance, etc.

*Legislative Series.*—One of the most important publications of the International Labour Office is its Legislative Series. This contains reprints of the text or translations of all laws relating to labour promulgated in the various countries. In addition to Acts and Decrees it includes administrative orders and regulations which are necessary to the comprehension of the application of the measures taken to give effect to legislation in the various countries. Each law is issued separately in order that the text or translation, as the case may be, may be available to those who wish to use it, with the least possible delay, and at the end of the year a complete collection carefully indexed is published in volume form.

Finally, the Office issues an International Labour Directory, which contains information with regard to the organisation and officials of the International Labour Organisation, a list of Government departments which deal with labour questions in all countries, and a full list of employers', workers' and co-operative organisations with various particulars. Lists are also included of organisations of intellectual workers and disabled men's associations, co-operative associations and various other organisations which deal with labour and industry in the various countries. The 1923 edition of the Directory contained 1,120 pages.

All the publications of the Office are issued in English and in French. A considerable number are also issued in German, and a monthly publication is produced in Italian and in Spanish. Some of the lighter literature of the Office is produced in eleven or twelve different languages. To undertake the mass of translation involved in the production of its publications the Office has recruited a staff of expert translators. The ordinary translator is a kind of Charon, whose duty it is to transport ideas, which to him are dead, across the waters of Styx. He receives on the one bank gibbering ideas, and when he has ferried them across, it is to a land which to the translator is, after all, merely a land of shades. Only when the translator is an expert interested in his subject does translation cease to be material transportation and become spiritual transfiguration.

In producing this mass of publications in such a variety of languages the Office has been animated with a desire to carry out the spirit of the Treaty of Peace. The peoples of the world need nothing so much as to be told of each others' success in grappling with the problems of labour and industry. If it is true, as Plato has said, that the man who most benefits the world is he who makes men acquainted with one another, then it may truly be added that the Organisation which most benefits the world is that which lets countries know of the endeavours and of the successes of others.

# CHAPTER X

## PROBLEMS OF THE PRESENT AND THE FUTURE

IF it be a sign of life to be faced with problems, the vitality of the International Labour Organisation cannot be doubted. Already, in the few years of its existence, problems of extreme difficulty have presented themselves for solution. While solutions have been reached—in some cases complete, in other cases provisional or tentative—it is abundantly clear that the years to come will bring with them, together with their harvest of results, sheaves of new problems, complex and difficult.

These problems of the present and the future may be grouped in two main classes. There are, first, questions of competence, and, second, questions of machinery. Further, each of these classes of problems includes quite definite and different categories of questions. For example, among the questions of competence are included three main categories : (a) to what kinds of persons does the competence of the Organisation extend ; (b) to what kinds of actions does the competence of the Organisation extend ; (c) to what countries does the competence of the Organisation extend. Among the questions of machinery may be mentioned: (1) questions affecting the machinery of the Conference, notably its periodicity ; (2) questions relating to the composition of the Governing Body ; and (3) a multitude of questions relating to the functioning of the Office itself.

In this chapter, therefore, predominantly from the historical point of view, some of the most important and the most interesting of these problems of the present and the future will be considered.

## I. Questions of Competence.

### (a) To what kinds of persons does the competence of the Organisation extend?

The most serious, perhaps, of the questions which have already been raised with regard to the competence of the Organisation relates to the classes of persons with whom it is competent to deal. Does its work extend to all, men, women and children, irrespective of their economic situation, or are its activities severely limited to certain well-defined classes of the population?

The wording of Part XIII of the Peace Treaty is not so explicit as might have been wished. But what legal text ever is explicit? Discussions have already taken place on the scope of the Organisation in this matter. The Preamble to Part XIII twice mentions the workers in general as those whose interests the Peace Treaty seeks to protect, and special reference is also made to the protection of children, young persons and women. An apparently narrower sphere is assigned to the Organisation in Article 427, which begins as follows: "The High Contracting Parties, recognising that the well-being, physical, moral and intellectual, of *industrial wage-earners* [1] is of supreme international importance," etc. . . .

From these texts it would seem clear that the Organisation is competent to deal with the conditions of employment of all wage-earning workers without distinction of sex. The term "wage-earning" is important inasmuch at it would appear clearly to exclude from the operations of the Organisation the individual producer, such as the small farmer or independent author, who are not wage-earning in the sense of having a contract to hire their labour to a determinate employer. Wage-earners include, however, not only manual labourers, but also intellectual workers, such as clerks, teachers and civil servants. All these classes of persons receive in compensation for the services which they render a remuneration which is in general independent

[1] Italics not in original.

of the immediate results of their work and determined in advance.  It would appear logical, therefore, to consider that the competence of the International Labour Organisation extends both to manual labourers and intellectual workers, and to all classes of such workers. The Organisation has not, however, been allowed to maintain unchallenged this interpretation of its competence.  That competence has, so far, been questioned, or at any rate queried, in regard to three specific classes of persons :—

(1) Agricultural workers        (2) Intellectual workers
(3) Emigrants.

1. *Agricultural Workers.*—It is in regard to agricultural workers that the hottest discussions have taken place in connection with the competence of the Organisation.  It might at first sight appear that no possible question could be raised in this connection.  Agricultural workers are most certainly manual labourers, and their position in many countries is very definitely one which involves the " injustice, hardship and privation " to which Part XIII of the Peace Treaty draws special attention.  When, however, the Governing Body communicated to the various States Members of the Organisation the Agenda of the Third Session of the International Labour Conference which, as we have already seen, included various questions relating to the conditions of labour of agricultural workers, a vigorous campaign was waged in more than one quarter to prove that the Organisation was not competent to deal with agricultural workers.

The initiative in this campaign was taken by the Swiss Peasants' Union.  It protested, on grounds of principle and expediency, against the competence of the Organisation, and a long correspondence took place on the subject between it and the International Labour Office.  The matter was taken up by the Swiss Federal Council, which at the beginning of the year 1921 requested the Governing Body of the Office to withdraw questions relating to agriculture from the Agenda of the Conference.

In France the campaign was even more vigorously pressed. Before the Conference, a resolution had been adopted by the Commission of Agriculture of the Senate, which addressed to the Government a memorandum in which the Government was urgently requested to give to its representatives to the Conference definite instructions to maintain the incompetence of the Organisation in anything relating to agricultural questions. The Agricultural Commission of the Chamber of Deputies submitted to the Government similar conclusions. The French Government, in May 1921, prepared a memorandum protesting on grounds of expediency against the inclusion on the Agenda of the Conference of the question of the regulation of hours of labour in agriculture. In a second memorandum, the French Government formulated a general objection on grounds of principle to the inclusion of agricultural questions at all.

As we have already seen, the question of the competence of the Organisation was discussed at the Third Session of the International Labour Conference and by a large majority the Conference maintained the view that the Organisation was competent to deal with agricultural matters. So strong, however, was the opposition to the competence of the Organisation, that the French Government after the Conference requested the Council of the League of Nations to submit to the Permanent Court of International Justice a request for an advisory opinion on the competence of the International Labour Organisation. The Council on May 12, 1922, requested the Court of International Justice to give an advisory opinion on the following question:—

Does the competence of the International Labour Organisation extend to international regulation of the conditions of labour of persons employed in agriculture?

Further, the French Government submitted to the Council of the League a supplementary question, which on July 18, 1922, was forwarded to the Court, as follows, with the request for an advisory opinion:—

Does examination of proposals for the organisation and development of methods of agricultural production, and of other questions of a like character, fall within the competence of the International Labour Organisation ?

The proceedings of the Court, of which the first public meeting was held on June 15, 1922, were too lengthy to be reviewed here. Their decisions were, (a) in reply to the original question :—

The Court is of opinion that the competence of the International Labour Organisation does extend to international regulation of the conditions of labour of persons employed in agriculture, and therefore answers in the affirmative the question referred to it.

And (b) in reply to the supplementary question :—

This question, for the reasons above stated,[1] the Court answers in the negative.

The main arguments which were involved in this dispute were the following: Those who maintained the incompetence of the Organisation drew special attention to the absence in Part XIII of the Peace Treaty of any special reference to agricultural workers. The conclusion they maintained was that agricultural workers ought, therefore, to be considered as excluded from the sphere of international labour legislation which was entrusted to the Organisation. This argument was countered by those who maintained the competence of the Organisation by urging that the very absence of the words " agriculture " or " agricultural " in Part XIII was, in fact, a confirmation of the competence of the Organisation. The terms employed in Part XIII are general terms and no expressions are used designating particular industries. For example, no mention is made of commerce, of inland navigation, or fishing, but the competence of the Organisation to deal with commercial workers, with inland navigation, or with fishing has never been questioned.

It was further alleged by the opponents of the competence of the Organisation that an indication of the

---

[1] The opinion of the Court on this question was given at some length. It makes clear that from its decision " it does not follow that the International Labour Organisation must totally exclude from its consideration the effect upon production of measures which it may seek to promote for the benefit of workers."

intention of the Commission on International Labour Legislation to exclude agricultural workers from the scope of the International Labour Organisation was given in the fact that a proposal to include among the general principles stated in Article 427 the principle that agricultural wage-earners should benefit from equitable labour legislation had been defeated by the Commission. The reply to this argument was that the Commission on International Labour Legislation had been led to reject this proposal precisely because it feared that if special mention were made in the Treaty of one particular class of workers, it might possibly be interpreted subsequently as an intention on its part to exclude other classes of workers not explicitly mentioned. Agricultural workers were therefore not specifically mentioned in the Peace Treaty, not because it was not intended that they should benefit by the provisions of international labour legislation, but precisely because it was considered that no question could arise as to their inclusion under the perfectly general terms of the Treaty.

A long discussion also took place with regard to the precise meaning of the words " industrie " and " industriel " which appear in Part XIII of the Treaty. It was universally admitted that the English words " industry " and " industrial " include agriculture and agricultural workers. It was maintained, however, that the French words " industrie " and " industriel " have properly a much more restricted sense, and that " industrie " in French was in effect restricted to manufacturing industry. After a very long philological discussion, the majority agreed that the word " industrie " in French in its most usual and proper sense does include, as does the English word " industry," agriculture.

In the end, as has already been indicated, the Court decided that the International Labour Organisation was fully competent in questions relating to agricultural labour.

2. *Intellectual Workers.*—The International Labour Office has concerned itself with the conditions of intellectual workers from the point of view of information,

and no official protests against its competence in this matter have so far been made. On the other hand, it should be noted that no proposal has yet been made with a view to the adoption of a Draft Convention or Recommendation relating to intellectual workers, and consequently the absence of a protest cannot be regarded as signifying complete acquiescence on the part of all interests in the right of the Office to deal from the legislative standpoint with the conditions of such workers.

The Office first devoted special attention to conditions of labour of intellectual workers in connection with the decision of the Assembly of the League of Nations to create a Commission on Intellectual Co-operation. On this occasion, the Office drew the attention of the Secretary-General to the interest which the economic situation of intellectual workers might present for this Commission.

The question was further considered in relation to a proposal made by M. Justin Godart at the Third Session of the International Labour Conference for the nomination of a Commission by the Organisation to study the economic situation of intellectual workers. The Office considered that it would be disadvantageous to establish two Commissions, one by the League of Nations on Intellectual Co-operation, the other by the International Labour Office on the conditions of work of intellectual workers. It was therefore decided that it would be preferable for the Office to collaborate in the work of the Commission set up by the League of Nations. The attention of the Secretary-General was therefore drawn to the difficulty of separating in the international sphere questions concerning intellectual co-operation from questions concerning the economic situation of intellectual workers, and the solution envisaged by the Office was communicated to him.

The Secretary-General, while expressing the opinion that the Commission of the League was not concerned with questions relating to the economic situation of intellectual workers, admitted the representation of the

International Labour Office on the Commission. It was agreed by the Governing Body in its turn that this collaboration would be sufficient to meet the wish expressed by the resolution submitted to the International Labour Conference.

The Commission held its First Session at Geneva from August 1–5, 1922, and decided to request the Council of the League to organise an enquiry into the situation of intellectual life throughout the world. It explained in its resolution that this enquiry should deal more particularly with the economic position of intellectual workers, and in this connection mentioned the possibility of securing the assistance of the International Labour Office. It was agreed that in order to limit the subject and to permit results to be obtained before the Second Session of the Commission, the first enquiries should concern musicians and university teachers. The International Labour Office was asked to undertake the enquiry so far as musicians are concerned. The results of this enquiry, which covered thirteen countries, were duly submitted to the Second Session of the Commission which was held at Geneva on July 26, 1923. At this meeting of the Commission it was decided that the results of this enquiry should be published and further enquiries were undertaken relating to the conditions under which intellectual workers labour.

3. *Emigrants*.—The question of the competence of the Office to deal with emigrant workers has not yet been seriously raised. There is evidence, however, of a disposition in certain quarters to cast doubt on the competence of the Office to deal with the conditions under which emigrants live during transportation. It has been maintained that emigrants on board ship are not workers, inasmuch as they are not working on a contract to supply their services against remuneration. In other words, emigrants are to be regarded, on this view, simply as private individuals travelling for personal reasons. It is clear that the whole question depends on the definition of the term "emigrant." Information on this matter was issued by the Office in 1922 in a

publication which contains a list of the definitions which have been given to the term " emigrant " in the majority of countries Members of the Organisation. It is clear from this collection of evidence that the principal characteristic of an emigrant is his intention to leave his own country and go abroad for a certain period of time with a view to domicile in the foreign country, there to earn his living. Similarly, the immigrant is in general defined as " a foreigner who comes to a country to look for work on its territory." These definitions, therefore, involving essentially the idea of travelling in order to seek work, would appear to make it result that the emigrant may be considered to be a potential worker.

It is true that the Preamble to Part XIII of the Treaty does not speak of emigration as such, and the only principle laid down in the Treaty relates to the treatment of immigrant workers. On the other hand, as we have already seen, the mere absence in Part XIII of the Treaty of explicit mention of a particular category of workers cannot be taken to be intended to exclude them from the provisions of the Treaty. On more general grounds it should also be realised that the emigrant before his departure is a worker and that the mere fact that during the brief period on which he is travelling he is not actually employed, does not imply that he loses caste as a worker. In fact, it would be accurate to consider an emigrant during his actual voyage as being an unemployed worker. It has never been suggested, nor, indeed, could it be suggested, that unemployed workers do not fall within the competence of the International Labour Organisation, and it is difficult to see why any exception should be made to this general rule in the case of emigrants.

It is of some interest to note that at the Twentieth Session of the Governing Body a brief discussion took place on the question of emigration in connection with the decision of the Italian Government to convene an International Emigration Conference. It was made clear by the Governing Body that the competence of the Office to deal with emigration was not intended to be in any sense challenged or questioned by the holding of this Conference.

### (b) What kinds of action is the Organisation competent to perform?

A movement has recently been increasing to regard the task of the Office as strictly limited. Those who take part in this movement warn the Office to beware lest in its action it should go beyond the principles laid down in Part XIII. They believe that the Office is entitled to take no action except in connection with the ratification of Draft Conventions and Recommendations, and they even maintain that the Office, through its activities in collecting information or making enquiries, is apt to exceed its functions. States are on the look-out for any encroachment on their national sovereignty. When they consent voluntarily to limit this sovereignty in treaties or international agreements, they do so in the belief that no further concessions will be demanded.

From these two standpoints, therefore, it is maintained that the Office should confine itself strictly to administrative work and should decline to take action of a kind which, even in the smallest degree, goes beyond the strict terms of reference laid down for it in the Peace Treaty.

There is, however, another point of view. Zealous friends of the Office maintain that it should become a centre for all types of social reform. They desire it to intervene on every possible occasion, proclaiming the principles of the Labour Charter, demanding respect for it, doing its utmost to secure the realisation of the provisions contained in it, even where such action lies outside the normal procedure explicitly provided for by Part XIII of the Treaty.

The policy actually maintained by the Office falls midway between these two extremes. On the one hand, it fully realises the necessity of extreme prudence in every initiative which it takes. The Office has always set its face sternly against any pretention to be a super-State and to impose, or even to seem to impose, its decisions on individual States. On the other hand, it is not considered to be consistent with the high functions conferred upon it by Part XIII to decline through timidity to respond to appeals to its authority and to act in virtue of the character for impartiality which it has gained and in a truly international spirit. It is this spirit which has inspired the Organisation in all its action, whether such action was explicitly provided for by Part XIII of the Peace Treaty or not. The activities of the Organisation fall into four main classes:—

   (i) Activities in connection with the Conference;
  (ii) Activities in regard to conciliation and arbitration;
 (iii) Intervention to secure particular results in individual States.
     and
  (iv) Intervention in the form of special enquiries.

(i) *Activities of the Organisation in connection with the Conference*.—The ultimate purpose of the International Labour Organisation is the establishment and the application throughout all the territories of States Members of the Organisation of a body of international labour legislation. The term " international labour legislation " is convenient in this connection, but it is necessary to indicate its precise significance. In point of fact, the Peace Treaty created in the International Labour Organisation, as has already been suggested, not so much an international legislative authority as a piece of machinery through which a certain degree of co-ordination might be secured in labour legislation throughout the world through the direct action of national legislative authorities.

It will be remembered that the only direct and explicit obligation resting upon Members of the Organisation is to submit the decisions of the International Labour Conference for the approval or disapproval of those authorities which are competent to deal with the matter within the particular nation. The mere fact, however, that each nation is under the obligation to do this is of importance. The significance of this obligation will immediately become clear when the procedure of the

International Labour Conference is compared with that of the Berne Conferences. In the case of the Berne Conventions Governments were not obliged to bring them to the attention of their Parliaments. In other words, in the last resort they were under no obligation to consult public opinion within their own territories on the matter. The founders of the present Organisation, however, attached the greatest importance to the play of public opinion, and it was precisely with a view to permitting public opinion to bring pressure to bear upon Parliaments in securing the ratification of Conventions that the stipulation was inserted in the Peace Treaty that Governments should be bound to submit, with a view to ratification or other action, to the competent authority in their countries all Draft Conventions adopted by the Conference.

In this connection, action on the part of the Office may, under certain circumstances, be effective. The Office has always regarded it as definitely within its competence to remind Governments of this obligation. It has, in the case of each of the Conferences, officially drawn the attention of all States Members of the Organisation to the expiry of the period allowed by the Peace Treaty for the submission of Conventions to the competent authority.

The Office has not attempted to bring pressure to bear directly on public opinion in any particular country with a view to influencing Parliament to ratify Conventions. It has considered that any such attempt would imply an unwarrantable intervention in the domestic affairs of a particular State.

The action taken by the various States to give effect to the decisions of the various Conferences has already been indicated in detail and it is unnecessary, therefore, to refer to it here.

(ii) *Activities of the Organisation in regard to conciliation and arbitration.*—The Peace Treaty itself made provision that the Office should, in addition to its work in connection with Draft Conventions and Recommendations, constitute a centre of international

14

conciliation and arbitration. This type of action was probably envisaged when the Treaty was made to speak of ;" such other powers and duties as may be assigned to it by the Conference," but apart from this somewhat vague reference, explicit provision was made in Articles 312 and 77, of the Treaty of Versailles, in Article 275 of the Treaty of St. Germain, and in corresponding articles of the Treaties of Trianon and Neuilly, that the Office should appoint independent members of the Commissions set up to regulate the transfer of social insurance funds in certain territories in which a change of sovereignty had taken place.

In accordance with the provisions of these Articles, action has been taken by the Office in the nomination of members to these Commissions. In response to a request of the French Government, the Governing Body of the Office, during its Sixth Session, appointed as members of the Commission for the transfer of Social Insurance Funds in Alsace and Lorraine, M. Moser, Professor of Finance at the University of Berne, M. Lindstedt, President of the Social Department, Stockholm, and M. Abbiate, Senator, Rome. The Governing Body communicated this decision both to the French and German Governments and as the result of the work of the Commission, the recommendations which it made were confirmed by the Council of the League of Nations and thereafter put into force.

A similar Commission, consisting of the same members, was set up in the same circumstances for the regulation of the transfer of social insurance funds in the territories ceded by Germany to Poland. The task of the Commission on this occasion was particularly difficult in view of the fact that the territories ceded, unlike the case of Alsace and Lorraine, had previously been attached, from the point of view of social insurance, to a number of different units now divided by the frontier. Eventually, the Commission reached agreed recommendations, which were unanimously adopted by the Council of the League of Nations and again put into effect.

A third Commission was subsequently set up to regulate questions concerning the social insurance funds in territories ceded by Austria to Italy. M. Moser and M. Lindstedt were again appointed as independent members, and in the place of M. Abbiate, who, owing to his nationality, could not be appointed as an independent member, M. Maingie, Professor at the University of Brussels, was appointed as the third member.

These Commissions have done extremely valuable if unspectacular work, and acting in a spirit of conciliation, have succeeded in solving questions of the utmost delicacy.

Action was also taken by the Office, on more informal lines, but with no less happy results, in connection with a threatened international strike of seafarers in 1920. The circumstances of the intervention of the Office in this case may be briefly recapitulated. It will be remembered that the Genoa Conference failed to adopt a Draft Convention providing for an eight-hour day for seafarers by two-thirds of a vote. Shortly after the Genoa Conference, the International Seafarers' Federation held its annual conference at Brussels from August 5–12, 1920, to consider the situation resulting from the failure to reach agreement with regard to hours of labour. A resolution was proposed in favour of an immediate international agitation with a view to arranging a general seamen's strike. An amendment was moved, however, and adopted unanimously, appointing a delegation to interview the Director of the International Labour Office and to ask him to arrange for arbitration between the shipowners and seamen. Failing such arbitration a strike of forty-eight hours was to be called in all ports. If after this manifestation the seamen's demands were not granted, a Strike Committee was to be created by the Federation to fix the date of a general strike and to carry it out. The delegation met the Director, who undertook to bring about a meeting between the shipowners and the seamen. Though fully aware of the immense difficulty of reaching an agreement, the Director felt that every effort must be made to prevent the disastrous consequences which would necessarily follow from a seamen's strike, however short its duration. He therefore communicated with the International Shipping Federation, which, after careful consideration, finally agreed by a majority vote to meet representatives of the International Seafarers' Federation to discuss hours of labour on board ship and to ascertain whether any ground of agreement could be found. This decision was taken immediately before the First Session of the Joint Maritime Commission, which gave an opportunity for the principal leaders of the shipowners and seamen to discuss in detail the proposed Conciliation Conference. It was agreed that the International Shipping Federation should attempt to secure the presence of the shipowners of all the countries represented at the Genoa Conference and that this Conference should take place at Brussels. The Commission unanimously agreed to invite the Director to preside over the proposed Conciliation Conference, and both sides expressed satisfaction at the possibility of conciliation being brought about by the International Labour Office.

This Conference took place at Brussels on January 25, 1921, under the chairmanship of the Director, and as a result two Commissions were appointed to consider the main questions at issue. The consequence of this conciliatory meeting was that a strike was averted which would have cost the world more in a week than the International Labour Office is likely to cost it in a generation.

The value of the Office in connection with conciliation was further emphasised by the decisions of the Committee which drafted the German-Polish Convention, signed at Geneva on May 15, 1922, with the object of guarding against any interruption of economic life as a consequence of the partition of Upper Silesia and ensuring the protection of minorities. The framers of this Convention fully appreciated the importance of labour questions in the Upper Silesia area. They therefore made provision, alongside of the Mixed Commission which was to supervise the execution of the various clauses of the Convention, for a Labour Advisory Committee to be established with the help of the Governing Body of the International Labour Office. This Labour Advisory Committee is set up for a maximum period of fifteen years, and consists of a President and ten assessors. The President and two of the assessors are to be nominated by the Governing Body, each for three years. The Governing Body has complete freedom in the choice of the President, with the sole proviso that the person appointed should be of neither German nor Polish nationality. The two assessors appointed by the Governing Body are named upon the recommendation of the two Governments interested and must be German and Polish respectively. If the Mixed Commission should deem it necessary to appoint a special secretary for the Advisory Committee, he is to be named by the International Labour Office in agreement with the two Governments interested.

The Governing Body, during its Thirteenth Session, decided to accept the functions offered to it by this Convention and appointed as President of the Committee M. Albert Thomas, and as assessors, M. Sokal and M. Sitzler.

It will be the duty of this Advisory Committee to advise the Mixed Commission on labour questions in Upper Silesia. In certain cases, as, for example, where there are disputes as to rights of association, it will be obligatory to consult the Committee. In others it will be optional. On some questions it is provided that the Mixed Commission shall consult the Advisory Committee as a whole; on others, the members appointed by the Governing Body, and on others, the members appointed by the two Governments.

There can be little doubt that the Office will in the future continue to be called upon in similar circumstances to choose suitable disinterested persons as mediators or arbitrators. In this way, the international impartiality of the Office is continually being emphasised.

(iii) *Intervention to secure particular results in individual States.*—It is possible to conceive of intervention by the International Labour Office with regard to industrial and labour conditions in a particular country not undertaken in pursuance of explicit provisions contained in the Peace Treaty, but in accordance with the general spirit of the tasks entrusted to it there. In the history of the Organisation, one such act of intervention has been performed with the best results.

The Governing Body, at its Session of October 7, 1920, was given information concerning the inhuman conditions under which children were employed in the carpet-weaving industry in Persia, in Kerman and the adjacent villages. Photographic and other evidence was placed before the Governing Body tending to indicate that children were deformed for life through premature employment in unhealthy conditions. The Governing Body, recalling that Persia, as a Member of the League of Nations, has undertaken under Article 323 of the Covenant to secure and maintain fair and humane conditions of labour for men, women and children, and that Persia was a member of the International Labour Organisation, instructed the International Labour Office to make friendly representations to the Persian Government with regard to these allegations.

The International Labour Office therefore addressed a letter to the Persian Government setting forth the allegations which had been made and the decisions of the Governing Body. It urged upon the Persian Government the desirability of completing as rapidly as possible an efficient system of industrial inspection, and requested that it might be informed of the steps which Persia had doubtless already taken in this respect and of any observations which the Persian Government might wish to make with regard to the allegations regarding conditions in Kerman. Subsequently, in view of the difficulties of establishing communication with Persia, and owing to the fact that no reply had been received to the first letter of the Office, the Office took advantage of the presence of the Persian delegation at the Second Assembly of the League to approach His Highness Prince Arfa-ed-Dowleh, first Persian Government delegate to that Assembly, and submitted to him the considerations put forward in the letters sent by the Office to the Persian Government.

The communication of the Office had laid particular emphasis upon :—

1. The excessive number of hours of work in certain industries;
2. The improper admission of children of tender years to industrial employment;
3. The absence of the most elementary sanitary provision in the arrangement of workshops;
4. The extremely unhealthy conditions in which women and children worked in the carpet factories of Kerman and in the neighbourhood, mainly on account of the unnatural position they are compelled to assume, which, in a few years, causes atrophy of the arms and legs, as well as other physiological complaints of all kinds;
5. The low standard of living prevailing in workers' families on account of the insufficient wages.

His Highness Prince Arfa-ed-Dowleh undertook to communicate with his Government on the matter in question and to lend his assistance with a view to expediting the response of the Persian Government in securing the adoption of such measures as might be required.

As a result of this action, a letter dated December 9, 1921, was received by the Office from the Persian Minister in Switzerland, enclosing a copy of a telegram from the Persian Minister of Foreign Affairs, stating that the Persian Government had taken steps to remedy the unsatisfactory conditions of labour to which the International Labour Office had drawn its attention. The telegram read as follows :—

Telegram 31 August concerning children and women working in carpet factories in Kerman :

Have the honour to inform you that pending definite measures on this subject Kerman local authorities, etc., have been requested to enforce the following articles :

1. Engagement of workers to be effected with complete liberty on both sides.

2. Eight-hour day.
3. Prohibition of employment of boys and girls under age of 10 years.
4. Permission for workers to leave the factory at mid-day for rest.
5. Provision for healthy sites and pure air for factories.
6. Preparation by local authorities of comfortable and suitable seats for women and children to allow work in normal positions, etc.

Authorities also requested to regulate wages and welfare of workers.

In this case, no suggestion was made in any quarter that the Office had exceeded its competence.

Intervention of a somewhat similar kind was suggested in another case of much interest. The General Union of Workers of Spain forwarded a complaint to the International Labour Office alleging various actions in restraint of freedom of association which successive Spanish Governments since 1917 were stated to have taken. This complaint was considered by the Governing Body at its Sixth Session on January 12, 1921.

In a statement made by the representative of the Spanish Government on the Governing Body, it was maintained that the facts to which the General Union of Workers referred fell within the scope of the national and internal administration of Spain and were within the competence solely of the sovereign, the executive authority of Spain. The Spanish Government therefore maintained that the Governing Body of the International Labour Office was not competent to judge of, or even to comment on, such facts. This point of view was criticised by M. Jouhaux on behalf of the Workers' Group. He urged that it was desirable that the truth or falsity of the allegations should be proved, and that this could only be done by making enquiry both of the Spanish Government and of the Spanish trade unions; and that if such an enquiry were made, it would not affect in any way the sovereignty of Spain.

After subsequent discussion, the Director explained the situation from the point of view of the Office. He pointed out that the Governing Body was faced by a difficult situation which involved the essential principles of the International Labour Organisation. In the case under consideration, it was impossible to have recourse to the action provided for under Article 409 of the Treaty and the following Articles as though the question at issue were the observance of a regular Convention. In such a matter the International Labour Office could only intervene, if at all, by way of an enquiry. Such an enquiry, however, could be undertaken only if the Government concerned acquiesced. In the case under discussion, Spain, one of the Members of the International Labour Organisation, declared that the questions at issue were of a purely domestic character, and in face of that refusal it appeared difficult to intervene.

On the other hand, the workers' organisations were also represented on the Governing Body, and they naturally were anxious to secure respect for the principles set up in the Preamble to Part XIII of the Peace Treaty and in Article 427.

The Director further emphasised the fact that the voluntary adherence of the various States was the essential principle upon which the International Labour Organisation was founded. When, for example, the question of the ratification of a Convention arose, it was clear that economic action could only be taken with regard to a State which failed to apply the Convention which it had ratified and not to a State which had refused to ratify a Convention. He therefore thought that as regards the application of general principles, unless States voluntarily agreed to apply them, the International Labour Organisation could not at present have recourse to coercive measures. Nothing in the Treaty of Peace authorised it.

On the other hand, it was desirable in all matters, such as the exercise of the right of association, to keep public opinion informed. If the forces of public opinion were thus constantly informed the future could be regarded with confidence.

In the end, the Governing Body decided, in accordance with the views expressed, that the Director should publish in the Official Bulletin an account of the discussion which had taken place, together with the letter of complaint, to which was annexed a detailed report submitted by the General Secretary of the General Union of Workers of Spain.

The general principles on which the Governing Body based its decision—on the one hand to respect sovereignty, on the other to bring the facts to the bar of public opinion—will undoubtedly guide the International Labour Office in such subsequent cases as may arise.

(iv) *Intervention in the form of special enquiries.*— In addition to the types of action above mentioned, other cases have occurred in which the Office has been called in in the cause of social peace with the full acquiescence of one or more sovereign States. In these cases the work of the Office has been confined to the field of enquiry. It is clear that the information in question cannot be collected and published without the entire approval of the sovereign State within whose territory the work is done. Where, however, the State approves, the facts brought together and issued by the Office as a result of impartial enquiry are of great value in view of the needs for which the International Labour Organisation was created.

A number of enquiries of this kind have in fact been undertaken by the Office.

*Freedom of Association in Hungary.*—On May 1, 1920, the Director of the International Labour Office received from Count Teleki, the Hungarian Minister for Foreign Affairs, a telegram requesting that the International Labour Office should send to Hungary as soon as possible a delegation composed of as many members as possible, to enter into direct relations with the leaders of the Hungarian workers and with the Hungarian Government, in order to form an accurate idea of the situation. The delegates would thus be able to convince themselves by personal experience that the continuous rumours of the alleged " White Terror " and persecutions of the workmen were grossly exaggerated. The Director of the International Labour Office informed the Hungarian Government that it belonged to the Governing Body of the Office to decide whether a delegation of such great importance could be sent.

The question was accordingly submitted to the Governing Body at its Fourth Session in Genoa, in June 1920. That this appeal for impartial investigation on the part of the International Labour Office should be responded to was obvious. It was evidence of the authority which the International Organisation, then newly formed, exercised even with a State that was not a Member of the League of Nations. On the other hand, it was impossible for the Office to undertake the responsibility of a Commission which would obviously be of a political nature, and which would, to some extent, have obliged the Governing Body to play the part of arbiter or judge.

The Governing Body accordingly decided that it was not practicable to appoint official representatives of the various groups, i.e. the Governments, employers and workers. Several members drew attention to the fact that the question before them was an essentially political one. They were apprehensive lest any interference on the part of the Governing Body should create an undesirable precedent, which might be quoted in the future by some political or economic party. They realised that a Commission sent by the Governing Body could not, from the very form in which the question had been put, play the actual part of judge, for which it had no competence.

But, taking into consideration that in accordance with Article 396 of the Peace Treaty " the functions of the International Labour Office shall include the collection and distribution of information on all subjects relating to the international adjustment of conditions of industrial life and labour " : and bearing in mind that Part XIII of the Peace Treaty mentions in formal terms, as one of the guarantees which must be given to workers, the principle of freedom of association, the Governing Body authorised the Director to send to Hungary upon its responsibility a certain number of persons to collect such information as the Hungarian Government or the workers' organisations deemed it necessary to submit to them.

The essential object of the enquiry was to examine the conditions imposed upon the trade unions in Hungary. Public opinion would judge from the evidence collected, whether the principle of freedom of association provided for in the Preamble to Part XIII and in Article 427 of the Treaty was being observed.

The enquiry, which was undertaken by three officials of the Office in August 1920, lasted several weeks. Valuable documentary information was supplied by the Government, by employers and by workers, and the members of the Commission had long and frequent discussions with the chief officials of the employers' organisations and the leaders of the workers' organisations, and with ministers and officials. The results of the enquiry, after having been submitted to the Governing Body, were published by the Office in a report under the title of "Trade Union Conditions in Hungary." The report undoubtedly helped the public to form a just and impartial opinion on a question which had given rise to keen discussion. Further, in Hungary itself the condition of the workers has, as a result of the enquiry, improved. The Hungarian Government has drawn up a memorandum which shows clearly that, after the enquiry undertaken by the International Labour Office, it adopted important measures on various points to which attention had been drawn by members of the Commission.

*Russian Prisoners in German Internment Camps.*— In a letter of August 17, 1921, the Executive Committee of the Conference of Members of the Russian Constituent Assembly laid before the International Labour Office certain protests concerning the state of affairs in Russian internment camps in Germany. Other communications on the same subject were received from the International Federation of Trade Unions on September 2, 1921, and a group of prisoners in the Lichtenhorst Camp on September 25, 1921. In each case it was suggested that the International Labour Office should undertake an enquiry, to be followed by a report on the living and working conditions of prisoners of war and the measures for their relief which might be taken or suggested to the High Commissioner appointed by the League of Nations.

On October 8, 1921, the Director of the International Labour Office wrote to the German Government informing it of these communications, and requesting permission to send a member of his staff to Germany in connection with the question. In reply, the International Labour Office was informed that the German Government accepted the proposal, and a representative of the Office arrived in Berlin on February 1, 1921.

From February 6th–14th, the representative of the Office visited the camps of Wünsdorf, Cottbus, Lichtenhorst and Zelle. He was able to converse freely with the prisoners and interned persons everywhere, as the German authorities gave him every assistance in order to facilitate his mission and allow him to obtain the fullest possible information.

On his return to the Office the representative drew up a report, which was communicated to the German Government. The Government approved its general tenor, but pointed out certain corrections of detail necessitated by changes introduced in the Russian internment camps since the visit of the Office representative. The modifications in question were fully in accordance with the suggestions made by the representative of the International Labour Office in the conclusions of his report.

*Compulsory Labour Service in Bulgaria.*—Under somewhat similar circumstances the Office was invited, on September 18, 1921, by the Bulgarian Government to undertake an enquiry into the application and results of compulsory labour service. The importance of the proposal was immediately appreciated by the Office. The question was one which had aroused much discussion both in Bulgaria itself and abroad. In Bulgaria, the reform had been stoutly contested as a matter of internal politics. Abroad, the Inter-Allied Conference of Ambassadors, which feared that the institution bore the stamp of militarism, demanded the introduction of an important amendment in the original text of the Act by virtue of the Treaty of Neuilly. The reform was interpreted by others as an application of Bolshevik theory. The International Labour Office therefore welcomed the opportunity thus offered by the Bulgarian Government of throwing light on the spirit, working and results of this new institution. It therefore instructed M. Max Lazard, President of the French Association for Unemployment, to proceed to Sofia in April 1922 to undertake the enquiry.

M. Lazard spent three months in Bulgaria and was given every facility by the authorities in the prosecution of his enquiry. The investigation was not confined to an examination of the Act itself, its application and its results. It viewed the institution also in its proper perspective in the light of the circumstances in which it originated. As the first impartial report on the question, it has been of value not only to the Bulgarian Government itself in its reconsideration of the methods of applying the Act, but also outside Bulgaria by enabling public opinion to form a just estimate of the real significance of this interesting innovation.

*The Eight-Hour Act in the French Mercantile Marine and the Eight-Hour Act in Czechoslovakian Agriculture.*—Brief mention may be made of two further enquiries in a severely limited field undertaken by the Office within individual States. It will be remembered that the Joint Maritime Commission decided during its First Session in November 1920 that an enquiry should be conducted on the subject of the working of the Eight-Hour Act in the French Mercantile Marine with a view to obtaining precise information as to the methods of its application. The French Government gave every facility for the prosecution of the enquiry, and in addition to supplying full documentary information, enabled the International Labour Office to send two of its officials to Havre and Marseilles with a view to obtaining on the spot complementary information. These officials also obtained information directly from the representatives of the local seamen's organisations, and a report was also contributed to the enquiry by the Central Committee of French Shipowners. All this information was brought together and published by the Office under the title of "Enquiry concerning the application of the Eight-Hour Day in the French Mercantile Marine."

The enquiry into the application of the Eight-Hour Act in agriculture in Czechoslovakia was undertaken in 1921, and is of special interest, in view of the controversy which took place prior to the 1921 Session of the Conference on the advisability of considering the question of the adaptation to agriculture of the Washington Eight-Hour Convention. In this case, the enquiry was not undertaken solely by the Office, but in participation with the Czechoslovakian Government itself. The Minister for Social Welfare in the Republic of Czechoslovakia thought it necessary to institute an enquiry in view of discussions which were taking place in Czechoslovakia itself. In November 1920, he therefore informed the International Labour Office that this enquiry would take place in Prague and invited the Office to send a representative. The invitation was accepted by the Office and a member of its staff was duly present at the enquiry. He subsequently studied the working of the Act on the spot, visiting several agricultural societies and collecting the evidence of representatives of landowners, agricultural workers and the Government.

The result of the enquiry was published under the title of "The Eight-Hour Day and its application to Agriculture in Czechoslovakia." It contains a detailed examination of the methods used for applying the Act, describes its results and discusses the social and economic changes to which it gave rise. The sole aim of the report was to give facts as accurately as possible and thus to facilitate the formation of opinion on the first experiment in the legal restriction of hours of work in agricultural States.

*Labour conditions in Soviet Russia.*—A somewhat special case, analogous in inception but not in results, was the enquiry into labour conditions in Soviet Russia. This enquiry was, in fact, not prosecuted in Russia itself, although it had been the intention of the Governing Body that this should be done. The proposal that the enquiry should be undertaken was made by M. Sokal, the representative of the Polish Government, at the Second Session of the Governing Body held in January 1920 in Paris. M. Sokal laid emphasis on the fact that the absence of accurate and impartial information on the labour and industrial situation in Soviet Russia had given rise among certain sections of opinion to dangerous illusions which were hindering the increase of production. At that time, it will be remembered, the cry in all the Western countries was for "production and still more production."

It was clear, however, that an enquiry of this kind raised a number of difficulties of a diplomatic character. The question arose how far the Governments of States Members of the Organisation would agree to an enquiry of the kind, and further, how far the League of Nations could be asked to assist the International Labour Office with the means at its disposal. No decision was therefore taken at this Session of the Governing Body.

At its Third Session, the Governing Body considered the results of enquiries which had, in the meantime, been made by the Director as to the procedure which might be followed, and it decided to send a Commission consisting of five employers' representatives, five workers' representatives and two Government representatives to study labour conditions and the position of the working classes in Russia. Arrangements were also made for collaboration with a separate Commission which was to be sent by the League of Nations.

In spite of long-continued negotiations, however, neither the International Labour Office nor the League of Nations obtained the permission of the Soviet Government to enter Russia. It therefore became clear that the projected enquiry could not be carried out in Russia itself. The Office therefore contented itself with publishing the information it had collected from documentary sources in two reports entitled respectively *Labour Conditions in Soviet Russia* and *The Organisation of Industry and Labour Conditions in Soviet Russia*.

The authority which the Office acquired as a source of impartial information on labour and industrial conditions in Russia has frequently subsequently been recognised, notably by the requests for technical collaboration addressed to it by the Genoa Economic Conference and by the various Famine Relief Organisations in Russia.

### (c) To what countries does the competence of the Office extend?

The territorial competence of the Organisation extends to all the States Members of the Organisation. Further, since membership of the Organisation is implied in membership of the League of Nations, the competence of the Organisation clearly extends to all countries Members of the League of Nations.

*El Salvador.*—One case has, indeed, arisen in which a State, a Member of the League of Nations, has claimed that this membership does not necessarily involve membership of the Organisation. The State in question is El Salvador. This State, in the year 1920, maintained that though it adhered to the Covenant of the League and thereby became a Member of the League of Nations, it undertook no obligations as regards the International Labour Organisation. No mention of the International Labour Organisation is contained in the actual text of the Covenant, and El Salvador has not signed the Treaty of Versailles whereby the International Labour Organisation was constituted.

15

Organisation should have the right to appoint an expert to the Permanent Mandates Commission who might attend, in an advisory capacity, all meetings of the Commission at which questions relating to labour were discussed. This decision has given the International Labour Office an opportunity of following closely the application of the Mandates and of drawing attention to the importance of not leaving mandated territories outside the scope of the system created by Part XIII of the Treaty.

The Permanent Mandates Commission, at its First Meeting, drew up a kind of questionnaire which would serve as an indication to the Mandatory States of the nature of the information which the Commission desired to receive in the Annual Reports which they are obliged to render. It was decided to include in this questionnaire the following question : " Have measures been taken to ensure, in accordance with Part XIII of the Treaty of Versailles, the taking into consideration of Conventions or Recommendations of the International Labour Conference?" Thus, the attention of each Mandatory Power was drawn by the Mandates Commission to the necessity of fulfilling in respect of mandated territories the essential obligations of Part XIII of the Treaty.

The Office is, of course, fully aware that many of the Draft Conventions and Recommendations cannot be applied in their entirety in areas where industrial organisation is practically non-existent. Part XIII of the Treaty clearly recognises that differences of climate, habits and customs, of trade and industrial tradition, may make strict uniformity in the conditions of labour difficult of immediate attainment. It is, however, true that in every country the beginnings of industrial organisation entail the greatest hardships on the wage-earning population. The Office is in a position to perform useful service not only in protecting these wage-earners, but also in safeguarding undertakings in the older industrial countries which might be affected by illicit competition.

## II. Questions of Machinery.

Problems have arisen with regard to matters of administration, organisation, or machinery, in the case of the Conference, of the Governing Body and of the Office. By far the most important and numerous of these problems are those relating to the constitution, composition and decisions of the Conference.

### (a) Problems relating to the constitution, composition and decisions of the Conference.

1. *The Periodicity of the Conference.*—It was laid down in the Peace Treaty, it will be remembered, that the Conference should meet at least once every year. Doubts began to be felt, however, after the first two Conferences had been held, as to the desirability of such frequent sessions of the Conference. Some held that the Conference had been proceeding possibly too rapidly in its programme of social legislation, and they were accordingly inclined to the view that bi-ennial sessions would be sufficient. This view tended to find support among the States which, because of distance, or the state of the exchanges, found that the expense of sending delegations to an Annual Conference was heavy. On the other hand, the opinion was strongly maintained that the adoption of a system of bi-ennial sessions would be taken to be evidence of an impairment of the spirit which had produced the Organisation, would lessen the importance of the Conference, and would frequently render it impossible to bring matters of urgency before it.

In view of the interest which was taken in the matter, the question was placed on the Agenda of the Fourth Conference. The Office proposed to the Conference a compromise between the two views which have been mentioned, according to which Sessions of the Conference would continue to be annual, but would be occupied in alternate years with more important questions instituting legislative action, while the intervening sessions would deal largely with internal matters and would enable the Conference to take stock of the progress that had been accomplished. This proposal of the Office was partially accepted by the Conference, and the decision adopted by it provided that the Governing Body should be requested to consider the suggestion that the Sessions of the Conference should be alternately of a preparatory and decisive character. The first of the series of two sessions would be devoted to the discussion of drafts for Conventions or Recommendations which would be approved by a simple majority vote, while the final recording vote for the Draft Convention or Recommendation in the manner required by the Treaty would be postponed till the opening of the succeeding Session. The advantages of this proposal were two. In the first place, no amendment of the Treaty was required, as would have been the case if it had been decided to alter the periodicity of the Conferences; and in the second, satisfaction was given to the feeling which had been widely held, and for which experience had shown there was some justification, that in the case of extremely intricate and complicated matters it would be well to adopt a more leisurely procedure than was possible under circumstances in which the whole process of discussion, drafting and adoption took place in the course of two or three hurried weeks.

2. *The Composition of the Conference.*—Another important problem which has given rise to difficulty is the composition of the Conference. It will be remembered that the Peace Treaty provides that each State Member may send a delegation consisting of four delegates, two being Government delegates and two respectively workers' and employers' delegates. Clearly, if Governments adopt the habit of sending incomplete delegations, the equilibrium of the Conference is not preserved. At the Washington Conference sixteen of the States represented sent only Government delegates. This fact called forth protests on the part of the workers' delegates, who considered that the posi-

tion of the workers at the Conference was thereby weakened.

The Commission on Standing Orders of the Washington Conference expressed the opinion that a positive obligation rested on the Governments to appoint four delegates and that in principle they might confine their delegation to Government delegates only if representative employers and workers organisations did not exist in their countries.

The problem is a complicated one.  On the one hand, it is certain that the absence of the proper proportion of employers' and workers' delegates alters the general attitude of the Conference and disturbs the equilibrium which should be maintained between the interests represented.  It is clear, on the other hand, that if States in which employers' and workers' organisations are in a rudimentary stage of development were obliged to send complete delegations, there would be a serious risk that the employers' and workers' delegates would be ill-qualified to represent the special interests of the employers and workers respectively.

The predominance of Government delegates was again marked at the Conference of Geneva in 1922.  Out of a total of 112 delegates, 68 represented Governments, 22 employers and 22 workers, whereas had the States Members represented sent complete delegations the numbers would have been 78, 39 and 39 respectively. Uneasiness was therefore expressed lest the Government delegates should, by the absence of their colleagues of the other two groups, assume greater preponderance in the decisions of the Conference than the framers of the Treaty intended.

The Conference decided that the Governing Body should be asked to examine the whole question and to report upon it later.

This question is still under consideration.  It is, however, clear that while it is of importance, in view of the reasons which have already been mentioned, not to give too strict an interpretation to the provisions of the Treaty, it is highly desirable that every State should realise, in the interest of preserving the balance of the Conference, the necessity of fulfilling the obligations laid upon it to send a complete delegation if the conditions of the organisation of employers and workers respectively permit.

No sympathy can be felt for the attitude recently adopted in certain South American States, according to which representation of employers and workers should be reserved for States in which a "class struggle" exists. They maintain that in "democratic States like those of South America," Government delegates should be sufficient. It is clear that an attempt to draw such a distinction between States in which a class struggle exists and between really democratic States would not only be a matter of extreme delicacy, but would be contrary to the whole spirit of the Organisation created by Part XIII of the Treaty.

3. *Workers' Representation.*—Serious difficulties have arisen on many occasions in connection with the decision as to the meaning which should be assigned to the term "most representative organisations" which have the right, it will be remembered, to nominate to their Governments the workers' and employers' delegates to the Conference. At every Conference some difficulty has arisen with regard to the credentials of workers' delegates. It will be sufficient here, however, to mention the two most important cases.

At the 1921 Session of the Conference, the Netherlands Government appointed as workers' delegate M. Serrarens, the General Secretary of the Federation of Christian Trade Unions of the Netherlands. Protests were made against this nomination by the Netherlands Federation of Trade Unions (the Socialist organisation) and by the International Federation of Trade Unions. The point at issue was whether the nomination of M. Serrarens had been made in accordance with the conditions laid down by Article 389. The facts of the case, which were not in dispute, were as follows :—

In the Netherlands, there are five federations of trade

unions, the names and membership of which on
April 1, 1921, were as follows :—

| | |
|---|---:|
| The Netherlands Federation of Trade Unions .. .. | 218,596 |
| The Federation of Roman Catholic Trade Unions .. | 155,642 |
| The Federation of Christian Trade Unions .. .. | 75,618 |
| The Netherlands General Trade Union Federation .. | 51,195 |
| The National Workers' Secretariat (on Jan. 1) .. .. | 36,038 |

The Netherlands Government tried to secure agreement
as between the five unions in the nomination of a
delegate. The National Workers' Secretariat, however,
refused from the outset to take part in any of the
negotiations. The second, third and fourth unions on
the list, all of which are Christian trade unions, agreed
among themselves with regard to the nomination, as a
workers' delegate, of M. Serrarens. In view of the
fact that the membership of these three unions together
is greater than that of the Netherlands Federation of
Trade Unions (the Socialist organisation), the Netherlands Government appointed the worker nominated in
agreement by the three Christian trade unions.

The Conference decided to admit M. Serrarens, but
in order that an authoritative opinion might be obtained
to guide the Conference in subsequent cases, it decided
to ask the opinion of the Permanent Court of International Justice. It therefore adopted a resolution
suggesting that an opinion should be obtained from the
Court as to the interpretation of Article 389 and as to
the rules which should be observed by the Members of
the Organisation in order to comply with the terms
of the Article in appointing non-Government delegates
and advisers to the Sessions of the Conference.

The Council of the League of Nations, which transmitted the request to the Court, realising, with the
Governing Body, that it was necessary to put to the
Court a specific case, asked for an advisory opinion as
to "whether the workers' delegate for the Netherlands
at the Third Session of the International Labour Conference was nominated in accordance with the provisions of paragraph 3 of Article 389 of the Treaty of
Versailles."

On July 31, 1922, the Court gave an affirmative reply to this question. In its opinion the Court refused to consider that the plural "organisations" employed in the third paragraph of Article 389 could be interpreted to refer only to the single most representative organisation of employers and the single most representative organisation of workers. The Court was of opinion that the only reasonable interpretation is that according to which the word "organisations" refers, in the case of countries where several industrial organisations exist, to the organisations which are most representative of employers and to the organisations which are most representative of workers. This is the essence of the opinion.

But having laid down this general principle, the Court insisted on three other points :—

1. The Court pointed out that the engagement undertaken by Members of the Organisation to appoint non-Government delegates in agreement with the industrial organisations which are most representative of employers or workpeople, as the case may be, is not, as had been maintained, " a mere moral obligation," but that " it is a part of the Treaty and constitutes an obligation by which the parties to the Treaty are bound to one another."

2. The Court insisted on the fact that the Governments should endeavour to reach agreement between the various organisations :

   The aim of each Government must of course be an agreement with all the most representative organisations of employers and workers, as the case may be : that, however, is only an ideal which it is extremely difficult to attain and which cannot, therefore, be considered as the normal case and that contemplated in paragraph 3 of Article 389.

   What is required of the Governments is that they should do their best to effect an agreement, which, in the circumstances, may be regarded as the best for the purpose of ensuring the representation of the workers of the country.

3. Finally, the Court pointed out that its remark could not in any way affect the powers of the Credentials Committee of the Conference :

   The Article throws upon the Government of the State the duty of deciding, on the data at its disposal, what organisations are, in point of fact, the most representative. Its decision on this question may, however, be reviewed under the seventh paragraph of this Article, and the Conference

has the power, by a two-thirds majority, to refuse to admit
any delegate whom it deems not to have been nominated in
accordance with the Article.  Such a refusal to admit may
be based on any grounds, either of fact or of law, which
satisfy the Conference that the Delegates have not been so
nominated.

These indications of the Court are undoubtedly
of guidance to States in the composition of their
delegations.

A further case of great interest, involving a somewhat
different problem, occurred at the 1923 Conference in
connection with the nomination of the Italian workers'
delegate.

The Italian Government had nominated as workers'
delegate the Secretary-General of the Confederation
of Fascisti Trade Union Corporations.  A protest was
made to the Conference against his admission, not on
the ground that the organisation he represented was
not the most representative workers' organisation, but
on the ground that it was not a workers' organisation at
all in the sense of Article 389 of the Treaty.

The Secretary-General of the Italian General Confederation of Labour (the Socialist organisation),
and M. Jouhaux, the workers' representative on the
Credentials Committee of the Conference, maintained
that according to printed documents which they quoted,
the Confederation of Fascisti Trade Union Corporations
was a mixed organisation including both employers and
workers with equal rights, and therefore, in the strict
sense of the term as used by the Treaty, it was not
a workers' organisation.  M. Jouhaux somewhat
facetiously suggested that in view of the constitution of
the Confederation of Fascisti Trade Union Corporations, if the delegate were admitted, the Italian
employers would in effect be represented by one and a
half delegates, whereas the workers would have to be
content with only half a delegate.

On the question of fact, information was officially
requested of the Italian delegation, which in its reply
to the Chairman of the Credentials Committee, stated

that "all the members of the directorate or secretariat
of the local unions, of the provincial federations, of
the national unions and of the national directorate
(secretariat, directorate and council) are workers " and
that "the Confederation of National Corporations does
not include any organisation composed of capitalists."

In view of this statement, which was signed by all
the members of the Italian delegation, the Credentials
Committee decided by two votes to one that the Confederation of Fascisti Trade Union Corporations was a
workers' organisation within the terms of the Treaty and
they therefore upheld the credentials of the Italian
workers' delegate. A debate took place on the subject
in full conference, and by a majority of 63 votes to
17, the report of the Credentials Committee was
adopted.

4. *Official Languages.*—A question of much less
juridical interest, but of considerable practical importance, is the problem of the official languages of the
Conference. By a standing order of the Conference,
French and English are the official languages. The
opinion has long been maintained in certain circles
that the German language should also be placed on an
official footing. The matter was discussed at some
length during the 1922 Conference. The pros and
cons of the question may be indicated rapidly. It is
claimed that German is the only language of a very
large number of the workers of Europe, and is further
the only secondary language current among many
others. This being so, it is urged that, if German
were accepted as an official language, the work of the
Conference and of the Office would reach an important
field at present relatively neglected. On the other
hand, the Treaty does not only not forbid, but expressly provides, that the publications of the Office,
which would include, of course, the documents of the
Conference, may be issued in languages other than the
official ones, and in point of fact many such documents
are so issued. The principal arguments in a contrary
sense are cost and the cumbersomeness of procedure

involved in two interpretations of every speech. Further it is argued that what is true of the German language is true also of the Spanish and Italian languages : that if a third official language be established, there can be no possible justification for excluding a fourth, a fifth, or even more.

The Conference in the end decided to maintain the present standing orders, according to which French and English continue to be the two official languages. It may be added, however, that every endeavour is made, by the publication of a daily account of the proceedings in German and in Spanish, to enable delegates who do not understand English and French to follow the main lines of the proceedings of the Conference.

5. *Ratification of Conventions.*—A series of problems of great juridical interest has arisen in connection with the procedure for the ratification of Conventions.

The first type of difficulty has been experienced particularly in France. In accordance with accepted constitutional procedure, the French Government requests parliamentary authorisation for the definite ratification of treaties or conventions only when such treaties or conventions have been signed by the plenipotentiaries of France and the other States concerned. The French Government, after having in the first place introduced into the Chamber of Deputies in April 1920 a series of Bills authorising the ratification of five of the Washington Conventions, changed its mind on the subject. It took the view that it could present to Parliament only Conventions regularly signed by plenipotentiaries, and it therefore undertook the transformation of the Washington Draft Conventions into Conventions conformable with French constitutional practice by carrying out an exchange of signatures with other States. Having secured the acquiescence of the Belgian Government in this matter of procedure, six Conventions which reproduced the texts of six Draft Conventions at Washington were signed at Paris in January 1921 by French and Belgian plenipotentiaries,

16

and a protocol was opened for the subsequent adherence of other States to these Conventions. A copy of this protocol and of these Conventions was communicated to the Secretary-General of the League of Nations by the French Government, together with a request that the exchange of signatures and the opening of the protocol might be notified to the other States Members of the International Labour Organisation.

The Office, consulted on the matter by the Secretary-General of the League of Nations, replied that in its opinion the procedure which the French Government proposed to institute was contrary to the spirit of Part XIII of the Treaty, and maintained that in adhering to the Treaty the States had bound themselves to follow the new procedure created under Article 405. This procedure, it was urged, was complete in itself, and an adequate substitute for the former procedure for the establishment and ratification of international conventions. The Office submitted that the characteristic feature of the new procedure, the absence of signatures, was an inevitable corollary of the whole organisation set up by the Treaty. The method envisaged by the French Government would result, for example, in differentiating profoundly between the position of the Government delegates and that of the employers' and workers' delegates at the Conference, a differentiation which is contrary to both the letter and the spirit of Part XIII. It would involve, further, the paradoxical consequence of obliging a Government, the delegates of which had opposed the adoption of a Draft Convention, nevertheless to cause that Convention to be signed by its plenipotentiaries in order that it might be submitted to the competent authority.

The Secretariat of the League and its legal advisers took the same view as the International Labour Office, and the Secretary-General replied to the French Government to this effect. If the Government found that constitutional difficulties prevented the direct presentation to the Chambers of Draft Conventions merely adopted by a vote of the International Labour Conference, it could open a protocol with States in the same position, but the League of Nations could not do so.[1]

The only States which have shown any tendency to follow the procedure adopted by the French Government are, in addition to Belgium, Luxemburg and Panama. It is clear, therefore, that the constitutional difficulty which is experienced in France is not of a general character. It would indeed appear that the French Government itself does not attach decisive importance to these questions of procedure. It has never in point of fact withdrawn the five Bills authorising the executive to ratify five of the Draft Conventions of Washington which were introduced into the Chamber of Deputies in April 1920.

A question has also arisen as to the methods to be followed in connection with the application of Conventions. Adherence to a Convention involves on the one hand its ratification, after, in most cases, the authorisation of Parliament has been given, and, on the other hand, the harmonising of existing legislation with the provisions of the Convention ratified. It is possible, however, that the modifications which must be made in existing legislation to bring it into conformity with the Convention involve changes in many laws. The legislative labour entailed may thus be at times very considerable, and may result in delaying the act of ratification itself. Should the act of ratification precede the legislative changes? Or should the State revise existing legislation before binding itself as regards other countries by the act of ratification? Various procedures have been adopted. In most cases Bills authorising ratification and amending existing legislation have been introduced simultaneously. It would seem to be logical to reform the legislation first, this being the essential thing, and to proceed later

[1] The correspondence exchanged between the French Government and the Secretary-General of the League of Nations, and between the latter and the I.L.O., was published in the Official Bulletin, Vol. II, No. 10, pp. 7–13 ; and Vol. III, pp. 655–662,

to the communication of formal ratification to the Secretary-General.

An extremely difficult series of problems has arisen in connection with proposals which have been made with a view to enabling States to ratify Conventions with reservations. It has been recognised that reservations of certain clearly specified kinds are permissible. These are reservations with regard to the formal articles of a Convention. For example, Bulgaria, in ratifying the Draft Convention on Hours of Labour, communicated a reservation with regard to the date on which it would come into force, and indicated that the provisions of the Convention would be applied to Bulgaria as from January 1, 1924 ; that is, that the ratification would in fact take effect only as from that date. No objection can be raised to a reservation of this type. The possibility of such a reservation was, in fact, explained to the Washington Conference by the legal adviser.

It has also been recognised that ratification conditional upon the ratification of one or more Members of the Organisation is permissible. This type of reservation is, in fact, implicitly justified by the terms of Part XIII of the Treaty, which recognise the obstacles presented by the non-adoption by a competing country of a given reform. No ratification accompanied by this kind of reservation has yet been received. It may be noted, however, that the Netherlands Parliament, in authorising the ratification of certain of the Washington Conventions, empowered the executive authority to communicate the ratification of the Hours Convention at such time as it should have been ratified by certain other States. The Office has pointed out to the Netherlands Government that the safeguards desired by Parliament in this case could be equally obtained by a conditional ratification, which would only come into effect when the ratification of such other Members of the Organisation as the Government might name in its reservation had been registered by the Secretary-General.

TH

authorities
probably
States, it
worked P
was felt
avoid this

At the
that a ne
future Di
amendmei
by a two
each dele
ratified tl

The w
during tl
amined tl
and was
problem.
to the Co
Conferen
thorough
to be su
least fou
has been
Session

In thi
text tha
1922, a
could
Convent

The
the forr
would
vention
majorit
delegate
cludes
authori
would
League

The Office has been consulted on the desirability of a third form of reservation, namely, as to whether it would be possible for a State to communicate a ratification conditional upon the subsequent adoption of legislation by its provincial Parliaments. In this case, however, it is not a question of a reservation which has regard to the attitude of another contracting party. The reservation would in fact be of the nature of a reservation with regard to the time at which the dispositions of the Convention should become operative. But such a reservation would seem only admissible if it is of a definite character. Otherwise the act of ratification, which is the act by which a State undertakes a solemn international engagement, would be a merely formal act of no importance, and would give no guarantee to other Members of the International Labour Organisation. A system of reservations, therefore, of the kind suggested, would seem to be contrary to the spirit of Part XIII of the Treaty, and would tend to hinder rather than to help the work of international labour legislation.

The question has also been discussed of the possibility of ratification with reservations on the essential articles of a Convention. This problem was raised by the Indian Government in informing the Secretary-General that in the case of the Draft Convention fixing the minimum age for the admission of children to industrial employment it had adopted resolutions recommending ratification with certain reservations. These reservations were the following :—

(a) That it shall not apply to factories employing more than ten but less than twenty persons unless the Local Government so direct ; and

(b) That transitional regulations shall be made regarding children between the ages of nine and twelve already lawfully employed in factories.

In a long and carefully reasoned letter the Office maintained that such a ratification with reservations on the essential articles of a Convention was not possible. It pointed out that no machinery existed for

the general acceptance of reservations once the Session of the Conference is over. It was therefore clear that if the procedure permitting ratification with reservations were admitted, it might lead to such a diversity of obligations on the part of the ratifying States as entirely to destroy the results of the negotiations of the Conference.

The Office drew attention also to the interests of parties other than the Governments concerned, namely, representatives of organisations of employers and workers. Since these representatives are parties in the negotiation of Conventions for which the Conference as a whole is responsible, it would seem that they should also have the opportunity of giving their acquiescence to a reservation. This would appear to be difficult unless the Conference itself should deal with the matter. The Office therefore concluded that the procedure of ratification with reservations was not contemplated by the framers of the Treaty, and would, if instituted, gravely damage the efficiency of the machinery set up by Part XIII of the Treaty.

6. *Amendment of Conventions.*—The difficulty which has been mentioned above, together with others which have arisen in the experience of three years, seemed to show the necessity for the adoption of some procedure to facilitate the solution of difficulties met with by States in their efforts to apply the decisions of the Conference through their national legislation. It has happened in many cases that a minor amendment to the terms of a Convention, in no way affecting the principle laid down, would remove obstacles to ratification by one or more States which may be desirous of ratifying but find themselves faced with minor difficulties of drafting.

The Treaty of Peace makes no explicit provision for the amendment of Conventions once adopted. The only procedure implicitly indicated would appear to be that of the adoption by the Conference of a supplementary Convention which would have to go through the ordinary process of submission to all the national authorities.  As such supplementary conventions would probably be of interest only to a small number of States, it would appear unwise to trouble already over-worked Parliaments with their consideration, and it was felt necessary to devise some plan which would avoid this.

At the 1921 Conference the suggestion was made that a new form of Article should be inserted in all future Draft Conventions, which would provide that amendments of this kind could be made in later Sessions by a two-thirds majority, including the majority of each delegation from the States which had already ratified the Convention in question.

The whole matter was submitted to a Commission during the 1922 Conference.  The Commission examined the various solutions which had been proposed and was impressed with the immense difficulty of the problem.  It therefore contented itself with proposing to the Conference a resolution which suggested that the Conference should instruct the Office to make a thorough study of the problem and to prepare a report to be submitted to Governments for observations at least four months before the next Session.  This report has been prepared and will be considered by the 1924 Session of the Conference.

In this report the Office examines and defends the text that had been considered by the Conference of 1922, and concludes that with one alteration this text could suitably be embodied in all future Draft Conventions.

The suggested Article dealing with amendments, in the form in which it is now proposed by the Office, would provide that amendments modifying the Convention may be adopted by the Conference by a majority of two-thirds of the votes cast by the delegates present, provided that such a majority includes the votes of all the Government delegates duly authorised to that effect.  Any amendment thus voted would be registered by the Secretary-General of the League of Nations six months after the close of the

Session during which it was voted, and would thereupon be considered to be incorporated in the Convention. If, however, one of the Members ratifying the original Convention should consider that the amendment adopted by the Conference required the approval of its legislative authorities, it would inform the Secretary-General of the League of Nations within a period of six months. In such a case the amendment would not be registered and put into force until it had been ratified by the Member concerned.

The main difficulty in such a proposal is that it would involve a delegation of powers. A Parliament in approving a Convention containing an amendment clause would in effect delegate its powers in view of the possibility of subsequent amendments. The executive power would be authorised in advance by Parliament to signify the consent of the State to amendments which might subsequently be adopted by the Conference.

It was considered by the legal experts of France, Germany, Italy, Belgium, Denmark, Roumania and Switzerland, represented at the 1922 Conference, that such a procedure did not involve any conflict with the system of public law of their countries. The legal expert of the British delegation considered, however, that such a delegation of powers would be contrary to the spirit of the British Constitution. In order partially to meet this difficulty and also other hesitations which had been expressed, it was agreed to include in the Article the provision to which reference has already been made, that Members of the Organisation should have the power to submit amendments adopted by the Conference to their Parliaments when they considered such a course necessary.

It is considered by the Office that the system of amendment submitted in this report is the only method by which difficulties arising in the ratification of Conventions may be removed, that it is not contrary to the provisions of the Treaty, that it protects the national sovereignty of the States Members, and that it is fully reconcilable with public law and legislative

practice in the various States Members of the Organisation.

From the point of view of the future of international labour legislation this problem is perhaps the most important of all those which have so far been discussed. Ratification of a Convention involves definite and serious obligations, for the non-fulfilment of which the Peace Treaties provide equally serious and definite sanctions. States naturally, and rightly, hesitate to ratify a Convention if they foresee that they will be unable to carry out even one of its minor provisions. Since, as we have seen, ratification with reservations on essential Articles is not provided for by the Treaties, the only alternative is non-ratification. While it is undoubtedly essential that the act of ratification should be regarded with all the solemnity which rightly attaches to it, it is extremely desirable that the greatest possible elasticity should be allowed with a view to facilitating the ratification of Conventions where some slight modification, resulting from circumstances or conditions unknown to the Conference which adopted them, would render this possible.

## (b) The Governing Body.

Two questions in connection with the Governing Body have given rise to difficulty. The first of these is the determination which are the States of chief industrial importance, and the second, the actual constitutional composition of the Governing Body itself.

1. *States of Chief Industrial Importance.*—It will be remembered that the Treaty of Peace provides permanent seats on the Governing Body for Government representatives of " the eight States of chief industrial importance." It lays down, however, no criteria by which industrial importance may be judged.

At the Washington Conference the places of the eight States of chief industrial importance were provisionally filled by France, Germany, Great Britain, Italy, Japan, Switzerland, Belgium, and, pending the adhesion of the United States, Denmark. Claims were, however, made either then or subsequently by Poland, Canada and India to a place among the eight States of chief industrial importance.

Endeavours were made by the International Labour Office and by the Council of the League of Nations, which is empowered under the Treaty to decide any question as to which are the States of chief industrial importance, to agree on criteria which would enable an unequivocal decision to be given. It appeared, however, extremely difficult to reach an agreement on the criteria to be employed, and consequently on the decision as to which in fact were the States of chief industrial importance. Under these circumstances the Governing Body attempted to avoid the difficulty by substituting for the eight States of chief industrial importance six States, namely, France, Germany, Great Britain, Italy, Japan and the United States. A Commission appointed by the 1922 Conference agreed with the proposal of the Governing Body, but the Conference, after hearing statements by the delegations of Canada and India, decided to maintain the provision of the Treaty that eight seats on the Governing Body should be held permanently by the eight States of chief industrial importance. These eight States are now France, Germany, Great Britain, Italy, Japan, Canada, India and Belgium.

2. *Composition of the Governing Body.*—Complaints had from the first been made by certain extra-European States that the representation of extra-European States on the Governing Body was entirely inadequate. In effect, the Governing Body, as appointed at the Washington Conference contained only three Members representing countries outside Europe. Much sympathy was felt on all sides with the extra-European countries in their desire to secure representation on the Governing Body. It was realised, in fact, that the International Labour Organisation could not be regarded as really international if seven-eighths of the Members of its Governing Body were drawn from one single continent.

It was therefore recommended by the 1922 Conference that an increase should be made in the size of
the Governing Body from 24 to 32 Members. A
new text was therefore adopted for Article 393 of the
Treaty. If this new Article is duly ratified, the composition of the Governing Body will be as follows :—

It will consist of thirty-two Members, of whom, as
before, one-half will be persons representing the
Governments, one-fourth persons representing the employers and one-fourth persons representing the
workers. Of the sixteen Government seats on the
Governing Body, eight will be held permanently by
the eight States of chief industrial importance, while
the remaining eight Members will be selected by the
Government delegates present at the Conference during
which the election takes place. Further, the demands
for additional representation on the Governing Body
made by extra-European countries are met by provisions
that six of the Government representatives, and two
each of the employers' and workers' representatives,
shall belong to extra-European States. This provision
will immensely facilitate relations between many of
these countries and the International Labour Office.

The new Governing Body elected at the 1922 Conference was necessarily constituted on the old basis.
Even so, it was found possible to give satisfaction to
extra-European States to this degree—that five instead
of three representatives now come from extra-European
countries.

It may be mentioned also as a matter of particular
interest to members of the British Commonwealth of
Nations that no fewer than seven of the twenty-four
Members of the Governing Body belong to this group
of countries.

### (c) *The International Labour Office.*

While the problems that have arisen in connection
with the organisation of the Office cannot compare in
importance with those that have demanded consideration in relation to the Conference and the Governing

Body, a peculiar interest attaches to them in virtue of the fact that they represent, in microcosmic form, two of the great difficulties of practical internationalism. International life is a delicate plant. International ideals have frequently assumed a Utopian form. International decisions have often been vague and shadowy. When these decisions have to be applied, when these ideals have to be realised, when this life has to be lived, who can wonder if it has been difficult to translate the vague into the definite, the delicate into the hardy, and the Utopian into the real?

The task of organising a new enterprise, always time-consuming and nerve-fraying, becomes Herculean in the case of organisations of international scope. Differences in national standards, customs, traditions, institutions and modes of thought and action, aggravated by differences in language, render extraordinarily difficult the speedy understandings and adjustments required in every administration. International co-operation, as exemplified by a Conference lasting two or three weeks, is considered, and rightly, to be a wonderful thing. Much more wonderful, though this is rarely realised, is the kind of international co-operation required in the permanent day-after-day collaboration of twenty-nine nationalities in the routine work of an Office.

In the history of the Office, two great problems have arisen. Though it would be rash to say that either has been solved, the approaches towards solution merit attention. The first of these problems relates to the fundamental principles on which the internal organisation of the Office should be founded. This is the problem of centralisation versus decentralisation. The other problem relates to the principles on which the staff belonging to different nationalities should be recruited and treated. This is the problem of uniformity versus diversity.

1. *Centralisation versus Decentralisation.*—When a new Government Department is established in a particular country, no question is raised as to the

general form of the organisation of the Department. There is a traditional system waiting to be followed. In the case of the International Labour Office, however, it could not be clear at the start what system of organisation should be followed. While each State has particularities, not to say peculiarities, of administrative organisation, all such systems may be regarded ultimately as variations of two types represented respectively by British and French Government Departments. And the great problem of the Office has been to evolve a scheme of organisation which would not merely be a compromise between these two methods, but would be an internally self-consistent system resulting from the adaptation to the needs of an international institution of the best elements in the two national schemes. The difficulty of the problem will become clearer if the chief characteristics of the two national systems are borne in mind.

The normal British Government Department consists of a Minister and Parliamentary Secretary, together with a Permanent Secretary, under whom are grouped several heads of departments. The heads of departments are responsible to the Permanent Secretary for the work done in their departments. All work done in the department is considered to be the product of the department as a whole, and for all this work the head of the department is responsible to the Permanent Secretary.

The normal French Government Department contains no Permanent Secretary, to whom the heads of the various departments are responsible. To a certain extent the functions of the Permanent Secretary are fulfilled by the " Chef du Cabinet " of the Minister. The " Chef du Cabinet "—a political appointment, changing with the Minister—in addition to ensuring the private secretarial work of the Minister, also acts as an intermediary between him and the various heads of departments. The result of this system is that the direction of and control over the various heads of departments exercised by the " Chef du Cabinet " in the name of the Minister is more fragmentary and spasmodic than the constant supervision of the British Permanent Secretary.

Further, on the French system, the team-spirit of departments is not strongly developed. The individual member of the staff who prepares a memorandum has a strong sense of *amour propre d'auteur*, and his Chiefs, even if they do not agree with his memorandum, tend to transmit it, leaving him the responsibility for what is regarded as his own individual work. On the English system such a memorandum would be modified and altered by each hand through which it passed, until in the end it could not be regarded as any one man's individual and personal work, but the collective product of the work of the department.

Lastly, on the French system, the heads of departments are in many ways more independent than British heads of departments. They have direct access to the Minister, through the " Chef du Cabinet," and questions at issue between the departments must be submitted for decision to the Minister himself.

When the International Labour Office was founded, the organisation partook in part of both systems. The Director, accustomed to the French system of administrative organisation, established in addition to the two main Divisions, the Diplomatic Division and the Scientific Division, a Cabinet containing a number of officials, and no fewer than eight " Technical Services," created for the purpose of advising the Director on certain important matters and to prepare reports and special studies on the subjects within their competence. Both the Cabinet on the one hand and the eight " Technical Services " on the other reported to the Director directly through his " Chief du Cabinet."

The British system, on the other hand, was exemplified in the strict hierarchic organisation of the Diplomatic and Scientific Divisions, and in the Central Registry and Despatch, which centralised all incoming and outgoing correspondence of the Office.

After eighteen months' experience of this system of

organisation, important changes were made. It had become clear that in an international organism, where centrifugal influences are often stronger than centripetal, it was essential to secure the highest possible degree of centralisation consistent with a due regard to the necessity of preventing the throttling of initiative by bureaucratic strangleholds. Accordingly, a third Division was constituted *pari passu* with the two already existing, and all the "Technical Services," together with most of the officials of the Cabinet, were placed in one or other of these three Divisions.

After a further period of eighteen months another reorganisation, this time on a less important scale, took place. It is important to note that the two most notable features of this second reorganisation carried still further the application of the general principle of centralisation. A Publications Section was established to centralise all work in connection with the preparation, printing, issue and sale of all the publications of the Office—work which had previously been divided between the three Divisions. And an Administrative Section was set up to assist the Director and Deputy-Director in co-ordinating the work of the three Divisions. Experience has shown that a high degree of centralisation is necessary in this international organism. The problem of the future is to ensure that this centralisation does not result in bureaucratising the Office. But who can doubt that a solution will be found for this new problem in international administrative organisation?

2. *Uniformity versus Diversity.*—The question whether it would be possible to secure uniformity in the conditions of engagement and conditions of service of members of the staff of the Office gave rise to considerable difficulty in the early months of its existence. It was necessary for the Office to grow very rapidly in the early months, and the difficulties of recruiting in haste an international staff naturally proved very great. In certain cases, Governments seconded members of their Civil Service for special

duty with the International Labour Office. In other cases, persons known to the Director and his chief colleagues were appointed. In yet other cases, recommendations were received from individuals in whom the Director reposed confidence. It was natural, therefore, that a staff thus recruited should be somewhat heterogeneous. A further element in its lack of uniformity was the fact that many of the officials of the Office were recruited in countries where the salaries of officials were extremely low. If they were to receive the same rates of salary as members of the staff coming from countries like the United States and Great Britain, where salaries are high, their salaries in relation to those obtaining in their own countries might appear extravagant.

These arguments, however, in favour of differentiating conditions of recruitment and work of members of the staff were counterbalanced by others of greater importance. Apart from the political difficulties which would arise from giving different rates of salary to officials of different countries, the system would result in remunerating equivalent service on a varying basis. Apart from the inequity of such a procedure, it was likely to give satisfaction neither to States with a depreciated currency, nor to States in which the cost of living was high. It was therefore decided, with a view to securing uniformity in the future, that at the earliest possible moment the recruitment of the staff should be by competitive examination. Thus, as early as December 1920, competitive examinations were organised in London, in Paris and in Geneva for administrative appointments.

The examination system is an absolute guarantee of impartiality and, in fact, it has resulted in the establishment of what may fittingly be called an " international civil service." Since this first experiment, the system has been universally followed and examinations have been held, in addition to the three centres already mentioned, in Rome, Bucarest, Belgrade, Warsaw and Prague. Uniformity has thus been ensured both in regard to the actual conditions of service in the Office and to the recruitment of the staff of the Office.

The general principles with regard to the conditions of work of members of the staff were established in the Report of the Commission of Experts appointed by the First Assembly which were approved by the Second Assembly of the League. The Report provides that the highest posts in the Office, that is, those of Director and Deputy-Director, should be filled by appointment from outside the Office and should be held for a period of not more than seven years. The subordinate personnel—household staff, copying typists, routine clerks, etc.—are recruited locally. The staff of the intermediate grades is recruited internationally for a long-term engagement, varying from twenty-one years in the case of administrative officials, to twenty-eight years in the case of clerks and shorthand-typists.

The unity of spirit represented by the staff has frequently been remarked. As evidence of this, it will be sufficient to refer to the Report of the Commission of Experts which stated that " all the administrative staff, without exception, are inspired by an unbounded faith in the great ideals of the League, by an unremitting zeal in the execution of its designs, and by an unshaken confidence in its ultimate success."

One problem, and that the most important, remains. This is the problem of securing the support of public opinion for the work of the Organisation. The machinery of the Organisation has been so constructed that its whole motive power is publicity. The need of publicity to keep the machinery in motion is demonstrated at every stage. Items are placed on the Agenda of the Conference because, in the view of important sections of public opinion, they require international examination with a view to the adoption of measures applicable in all industrial countries. And when a Draft Convention has been adopted by the Conference, it is again on public opinion, in the last resort, that it depends to secure its submission to

17

Parliament with a view to the enactment of national legislation. The Conference was not given sovereign power to legislate partly because it was believed by the framers of the Treaty that Draft Conventions unanimously adopted by an International Conference would be invested with such great moral authority that public opinion in the various countries would hesitate not to ratify them. Finally, it is on the effective power of publicity that the whole system of sanctions depends. Reasonable watchfulness on the part of those who are interested in the application of a Convention can make it certain that no serious evasion of its provisions can pass unnoticed, and every interested party has some avenue of access to the International Labour Office. The Office, in its turn, must give the fullest publicity to any complaint which seems to be reasonably well founded. Publicity is a new sanction in international affairs, and it could hardly fail, if due use were made of it, to be effective.

The support of public opinion is also essential to the Office in its daily work. The Office was frankly told by Lord Burnham, as President of the Third Session of the Conference, that it was its duty to educate the public as to the value of its work. He urged the Office " not to advance behind a smoke-screen," and insisted on the necessity that everything possible should be done to ensure that the activities of the International Labour Organisation should be known as they deserve to be known.

Public opinion may often be deceived ; in the past it has sometimes supported movements that have afterwards been found to be mistaken, and there is no certainty that in the future it may not again yield to the guidance of blind passion. But amid all the uncertainties of the post-war world, where all beliefs, all conventions, all standards are in flux, the brightest element of hope for the peace of the world seems to lie in the education of public opinion to a higher sense of social justice. It is with this conviction that the International Labour Office has adopted as its motto

" *Si vis pacem, cole justitiam.*"    And it will probably be found that not the least of the successes of the International Labour Organisation, from the standpoint of the maintenance of the peace of the world, is to have brought together the West and the East to work in harmony for the international realisation of social justice.

# BIBLIOGRAPHICAL NOTE

THE reader who wishes to study in greater detail the constitution and work of the International Labour Organisation will find the necessary documentary information in the following publications of the International Labour Office :—

(1) Constitution and Rules.

(2) Stenographic Record of the International Labour Conference : 1919, 1920, 1921, 1922, 1923.

(3) Official Bulletin.

A full bibliography, including all works which have appeared throughout the world on the International Labour Organisation, is published annually as an Appendix to the *Report of the Director* presented each year to the International Labour Conference.

# INDEX

*Printed in Great Britain by*
UNWIN BROTHERS, LIMITED, LONDON AND WOKING

GEORGE ALLEN & UNWIN LTD.
LONDON: 40 MUSEUM STREET, W.C. 1
CAPE TOWN: 73 ST. GEORGE'S STREET
SYDNEY, N.S.W.: 218-222 CLARENCE STREET
WELLINGTON, N.Z.: 110-112 LAMBTON QUAY